FREEFALL

Leadership Lessons from the Skies

BY

DARA KIERNAN

Visit the Official Website at: https://kpiconsultingireland.com

Printed in the United States of America

First Printing: September 2024

KPI Services Publishing

Hardcover ISBN: 978-1-0687737-0-9
Paperback ISBN: 978-1-0687737-1-6
Audiobook ISBN: 978-1-0687737-2-3

This book may be purchased for educational, business or sales promotional use. Special discounts are available on quantity purchases. For more information, please call or write.

Telephone: +353 87 328 6335 **Email: dara@kpiconsultingireland.com**

DISCLAIMER

While the author and publisher have strived to be as accurate and complete as possible in the creation of this book, readers are cautioned to rely on their own judgment about their individual circumstances to act accordingly.

The author and publisher are providing this information on an educational basis and will not be liable for damages arising out of, or in connection with, the use of the content in this book. This is a comprehensive limitation of liability that applies to all damages of any kind, including (without limitation) compensatory; direct, indirect or direct, indirect or consequential damages; loss of data, income or profit; loss of or damage to property and claims of third parties.

While all attempts have been made to verify information provided in this publication, the author and publisher assumes no responsibility for errors, omissions, or contrary interpretation of the subject matter herein. Any perceived slights of specific persons, peoples, or organizations are unintentional. This book details the author's own personal experiences and opinions.

You understand that this book is not intended as a substitute for consultation with a licensed professional. In the event you use any of the information in this book for yourself, which is your constitutional right, the author and publisher assume no responsibility for your actions or outcomes.

DEDICATION

To Michelle, my loving wife, whose unwavering support, patience, and encouragement have been the foundation of everything I do. Your love is my anchor, and your belief in me fuels every leap I take.

To Ethan, my dear son, whose curiosity, energy, and boundless spirit remind me daily of the joy of discovery and the thrill of adventure. May you always chase your dreams with the same fearless enthusiasm.

This book is for both of you, with all my love.

CONTENTS

INTRODUCTION

In 1994, at the age of 24, I did my first skydive. I'll always remember as the aircraft climbed higher, the world below transformed into a distant, serene landscape, while a whirlwind of fear and excitement surged within me. This mix of emotions mirrored the experience of new leaders stepping into their roles; terrified yet determined to succeed. As the altitude increased, my fear began to subside, much like the initial apprehension that fades as a leader gains confidence. When the moment of truth arrived and we jumped, the rush of freefall was overwhelming, yet the guidance of my instructor provided reassurance, akin to the support mentors offer to first-time leaders. Finally, as the parachute deployed, the chaos gave way to calm, mirroring how the initial challenges of leadership eventually give rise to a more controlled and confident approach. Just as the descent allowed me to fully appreciate the beauty of the landscape, so too does experience allow new leaders to see the bigger picture and lead with greater clarity and purpose.

A friend of mine and I went to County Offaly in Ireland to a small village by the name of Clonbullogue, the home of the Irish Parachute Club. I was terrified of heights but more terrified that this fear would hold me back sometime in the future, so I wanted to challenge myself and see if a test from the highest of heights would allow me to overcome my fears.

I have always been like this and in leadership I believe it has become one of my strongest attributes. The number of occasions where I have been required to do something in my role as a leader that put the fear of God into me are too numerous to count. Whether it was a difficult conversation with an employee or a decision that needed to be made, a conflict that needed to be resolved or a fear of failing, I would always tackle the obstacle face on. And although I've made my mistakes, and more than one I must admit, I have learned throughout the years and have sometimes needed to adapt my approach. But I have never shied away from what scares me. Overcoming fear as a leader is a critical step in a leadership career.

Clonbullogue was, and still is, a one-horse town. One pub, one B&B, a few houses, and endless fields where you could pitch a tent if you couldn't afford the £10 Billy Murphy would charge to stay in his B&B. In 1994, my friend and I needed to stay in Clonbullogue over the course of a few weeks because the weather prevented us from doing our skydive. We stayed with Billy each weekend until my friend, after a prolonged stay in the local pub the previous night, left the contents of his stomach in one of Billy's beds. We escaped that morning after some breakfast without saying a word about the indiscretion Billy would be sure to find as he cleaned my friend's room. To be honest, we were both more afraid of Billy shouting at us, because he was such a lovely man, than we were of the upcoming skydive that we were sure to do that day.

The weather was perfect. It was going to happen today, and as we arrived at the drop zone, I kept looking over my shoulder expecting to see Billy Murphy chasing us down with the soiled bedsheets. We jumped that day and I never saw Billy again. Well, not for another 4 years, and we'll talk about that later.

A number of months prior to this day, both my friend and I had applied for sponsorship cards to do a charity skydive. This was the cheapest and easiest way to do a skydive for free. As far as I can remember, all we needed was to get sponsored for £300 each and the skydive was free. We received our cards in the post, met each other in the pub that night to discuss a plan and show each other the cards we'd received, got very excited about the prospect of doing a skydive, and had lots of pints of Guinness. The following morning, I put the sponsorship card on my bedside locker, so that I wouldn't forget about it, and there it stayed until a week before the time the sponsorship was due.

Every day I would look at the card, and every day I would say "I'll get started on that tomorrow". Slowly but surely, however, I began to run out of tomorrows. Even though we both thought it should be easy, I really didn't want to have to ask people to sponsor me, if I'm honest.

We'd both agreed that all it would take is 30 people giving us a tenner each and that should be quite easy. There were a couple of problems with this logic, and granted, the logic had originated during a night of sipping Guinness and talking nonsense about how brave we were, and all the other nonsense 24-year-old men talk about when they're in the pub. Here were some of the problems:

- We both knew the same people. This meant that the 30 people who we had believed would give us a tenner would now have to give us a tenner each, making it £20, and therefore, they only gave us a fiver each knowing that they were going to have to sponsor both of us. This lack of planning now meant that we would probably need to ask 60 people for sponsorship.
- Some people just said "No". Not for one moment did we believe that people wouldn't be as interested in this as we were.
- Laziness. We never planned for our pure laziness and not putting the work into it. I'd love to expand on this issue, but that first sentence says it all.

As young, and quite possibly as stupid as we were, we kept putting off the inevitable, until we ran out of time. Eventually, I managed £35 in sponsorship and my friend managed £50, and that's only because his dad gave him £20 and mine gave me £5. After the skydive I asked my dad why he had only given me a fiver and his response was, "I had assumed that other idiot friend of yours was going to ask me too". To my regret, when I spoke with my friend's dad later as well, he said the same thing and had been expecting me to ask him, but I didn't because I thought that he'd given everything he could. Neither of us asked the other's dad. We had both decided not to, due to our assumption about the amount that had already been given. I thought it would be too much to ask for £20, and my friend thought it was too much to ask my dad if all he could afford to give me was a £5. We both assumed incorrectly, and it cost us.

Leadership Lesson – Assumptions

Assumptions can be costly in leadership too, for several reasons. Not only can it affect the company financially but making assumptions in leadership can affect various aspects of an organisation, including its culture, performance, and strategic direction.

Here are some key points explaining why:

- **Miscommunication and Misunderstanding:**
  Leaders who make assumptions or have preconceived notions about what others know, understand, or mean can lead to miscommunication and misunderstandings. This can result in tasks being performed incorrectly, objectives not being met, or conflicts arising within teams, all of which can be costly to rectify and can diminish morale.

- **Missed Opportunities:**
  Assuming that you know what staff need, what customers want or what the market needs without adequate research or feedback can lead to missed opportunities, not to mention money wasted on products/production or services that might not meet the actual needs of the target audience, leading to lower employee and customer confidence, poor sales and lost market share.

- **Erosion of Trust:**
  When leaders make assumptions about individuals' capabilities or intentions without seeking clarity, it can lead to mistrust. For instance, assuming an employee is not working hard enough without understanding their challenges can demotivate and disengage them, potentially leading to high turnover, which is costly in time and money spent on interviewing, training and integrating new employees.

- **Poor Decision Making:**
  Assumptions can lead to decisions based on incomplete or incorrect information. This can be particularly costly if it affects strategic direction and execution, investments, or operational changes. The consequences might include financial losses, wasted resources, and having to backtrack on decisions made.

- **Cultural Impact:**
  Assuming all employees respond uniformly to certain incentives, feedback, work style, and/or management styles can negatively impact organisational culture. This can lead to a lack of inclusivity, reduced innovation, and employees feeling undervalued or misunderstood, affecting overall productivity and engagement.

- **Risk and Compliance Issues:**
  Leaders making assumptions about regulatory compliance without thorough verification can lead to legal issues, fines, and reputational damage. Compliance requires precise adherence to laws and regulations, and assumptions can be both risky and costly.

- **Resource Misallocation:**
  Assumptions about project timelines, costs, or outcomes can lead to misallocation of resources. Overestimating or underestimating project needs can result in budget overruns, wasted resources, project failures, or employee frustration and burnout.

- **Impact on Leadership Credibility:**
  When leaders make assumptions that prove to be incorrect it can damage their credibility and authority. Recovering from such mistakes can be challenging and time-consuming affecting the leader's ability to guide and influence their team effectively.

To mitigate the costs associated with making assumptions, leaders should cultivate a culture of open communication and authenticity, seek diverse perspectives, engage in active listening, and make decisions based on data and evidence rather than conjecture. Encouraging a feedback-rich environment and being open to being challenged can also help leaders avoid the pitfalls of assumptions. Ensure you have done your research and make your decision on data rather than feelings. In the case of asking our fathers for money, we both felt that they were not our ideal customers purely based on their previous behaviour – we considered no other information (data) when coming to that decision.

We were also lazy, and we were distracted by the excitement of the upcoming skydive. We had practically done the skydive in our minds before we had ever put the steps of preparation in place. An analogy often used in soccer is that the striker had already scored the goal before controlling the pass which led to a sliced shot and a missed goal opportunity. Take every step one at a time and although it can be easy to run before walking, follow a logical process and don't make the mistakes we made.

Leadership Lesson – Procrastination

Procrastination in leadership refers to the delay or postponement of decisions, actions, or tasks that are critical to achieving a goal or crucial to an organisation's success. This behaviour can have several costly consequences for both the leader and the organisation.

Here are some of the key reasons why procrastination in leadership can be particularly detrimental:

- **Missed Opportunities:**
  Delaying decision-making can lead to missed opportunities. In the fast-paced, ever-evolving business world being slow to act can mean losing out to competitors, missing the chance to innovate, or failing to capitalize on market trends. This can result in lost revenue and diminished market share.

- **Decreased Productivity:**
  Procrastination can lead to inefficiencies and decreased productivity. When leaders delay it often causes a domino effect, stalling projects and demotivating team members. This can lead to missed deadlines, poor performance, and, ultimately, financial losses.

- **Increased Stress and Burnout:**
  Delaying important tasks and decisions can create a backlog of work, not just for the leader but for their team as well. This can increase stress levels and lead to burnout, affecting the well-being of employees and the overall health of the organisation.

- **Erosion of Trust and Credibility:**
  Leaders are expected to guide their teams and make timely decisions. Procrastination can erode trust and credibility among team members,

stakeholders, and customers. If a leader is perceived as indecisive or unreliable it can undermine their authority and weaken team cohesion.

- **Poor Decision-Making:**
  Procrastination often leads to making decisions under pressure, which can result in poor judgment, suboptimal choices, and rushed decisions that may not consider all aspects or potential consequences, leading to costly mistakes and corrective actions down the line.

- **Impact on Organisational Culture:**
  A leader's behaviour sets the tone for the organisation. Procrastination at the leadership level can foster a culture of delay and complacency affecting overall organisational performance and adaptability.

- **Resource Wastage:**
  Delaying decisions or actions can lead to resource wastage. For example, holding onto underperforming assets for too long, not reallocating resources efficiently, or delaying the termination of unprofitable projects can have significant financial implications.

- **Reputational Damage:**
  In instances where procrastination affects customer-facing decisions or product quality it can lead to reputational damage. This can have long-term consequences on brand loyalty, customer trust, and overall competitive positioning.

To combat procrastination leaders should adopt strategies such as prioritising tasks, setting clear deadlines, delegating effectively, and breaking larger projects into manageable steps. Emphasising accountability, fostering a proactive culture, and seeking feedback can also help leaders overcome procrastination and its costly impacts.

There were many other mistakes we made whilst only in the planning stages of our skydive adventure, and many of these mistakes will be discussed in further chapters. But for now let me tell you about the first of my many skydives, how I got hooked, and the lessons that came from it.

However, if we had done our research diligently, we would have discovered that it was possible to pay for this skydive experience rather than collecting sponsorship. I needed to add £265 to my sponsorship card, and my friend added £250 so that we would achieve the goal of £300 each. The price of this skydive package without sponsorship was, as far as I recall, £195.

Seriously, if the parachute club had only realised how stupid the two of us were they probably would have refused to allow us to jump out of a perfectly good airplane. Alas they did allow us. The charity received some extra funds, and the parachute club would soon refer to one of their members as 'Dead Man Walking'.

CHAPTER 1

LEAP INTO LEADERSHIP

My First Skydive

It was a Sunday morning after a bit of a heavy night in the local bar the night before and a 'ninja' type exit from the B&B we stayed in, when we arrived at the drop zone. The weather was perfect, and we both knew today was the day. Despite my friend feeling slightly under the weather himself, we were eager to go. I asked him how he was feeling, and he said, "Not the worst now – I think I left all the badness in one of Billy's beds, but just don't remember doing it".

As we arrived at the club the air was thick with anticipation, a tangible electricity that seemed to buzz through everyone present. Fellow skydivers shared knowing glances and encouraging smiles, a silent camaraderie among strangers bound by the common pursuit of a thrill.

We had been here before over the past few weekends. And we had experienced this excitement before, but because of the weather, our excitement was short-lived on every previous occasion, and our jumps were postponed. But today looked like it could be the day. Aside from our training, which was brief, we had also learnt many things about the weather from our previous visits.

The weather plays a significant role in the lives of skydivers around the world however the Irish skydivers are particularly affected by it. It rains a lot in Ireland. I've often thought that Irish people should have been born with webbed feet to stop us getting stuck in the mud, but alas we have the same feet as everyone else. Ours are just a little wetter.

Ireland also suffers from a lot of cloud cover and medium strength winds. All of these elements are detrimental to the safety of those who wish to skydive, for many obvious and perhaps not so obvious reasons. However I don't wish to use this book as a guide to safely fall from a plane.

Around the drop zone everyone spends their time either drinking tea or standing outside looking up at the sky. Not only are they looking at the people freefalling to the ground, they are also looking at the weather. Everyone becomes an expert meteorologist, possibly at the same speed as those folks in every Irish bar during the Winter Olympics when the 'sliding down a hill on your bum' event comes on TV. All that can be heard from a bunch of heavy drinking, overweight, whiskey-nosed men is, "I just don't understand how he forgot to point his toes... he'll never win a medal like that", to which another pipes up, "Don't be an eejit, it's his run up that's the problem, and he probably didn't grease his arse properly".

The skydiver's knowledge of weather is slightly better, but isn't based on any significant training or education; rather it's based on experience and a few broken bones along the way.

So we too had learnt from their experiences. Skydivers are wonderful people who love to share stories and experiences, who are so focused on safety and who are also extremely crazy. And so much fun. Although we had only been at the club for a few weekends it felt as though we were already a part of the team. They had a great social life and every weekend was like a party, to the extent that the majority of the expense came from the nights in the local bar and afterwards (no further detail will be divulged in this book, but I'm sure you understand). However each morning their professionalism returns; any sign of weariness from the previous night will prevent you from getting in a plane until they felt it was safe for you to do so.

I learnt so much from this community about inducting new team members into businesses. Welcoming new members into a team with the same warmth and inclusivity as skydivers do with their newcomers can significantly enhance team cohesion and productivity. Skydiving clubs are known for their strong sense of community, trust, and mutual support—qualities that are equally valuable in a workplace setting.

Leadership Lesson – Welcoming new team members

Here are strategies leaders can employ to make new staff feel welcome and integrated into their teams, drawing inspiration from the skydiving world:

Foster a Culture of Openness and Inclusivity

- **Skydiving Insight:** Skydiving clubs often host social events and debriefs after jumps where everyone is invited to share their experiences and learn from each other.
- **Workplace Application:** Create a welcoming environment where new employees are encouraged to share their ideas and experiences. Regular team meetings or informal get-togethers can help facilitate this. Engage in inclusive team "debriefs" at the successful conclusion of particularly difficult or long projects, and give kudos liberally, pointing out specific areas of exceptionalism.

Pair Newcomers with Mentors

- **Skydiving Insight:** New skydivers are often paired with experienced ones, providing them with direct, personal guidance.
- **Workplace Application:** Assign a mentor or buddy to new staff members. This not only provides them with a go-to person for questions and guidance but also helps in building interpersonal relationships within the team.

Emphasize the Importance of Trust

- **Skydiving Insight:** Trust is paramount in skydiving especially when it comes to safety. This trust in each other's abilities fosters a strong bond among team members.
- **Workplace Application:** Encourage an environment where team members feel confident in the abilities of their colleagues and leadership. This can be achieved through team-building activities that require collaboration and reliance on each other's strengths. Never diminish someone's efforts. Instead, seek to understand why they were ineffective as it may have been a simple lack of understanding what was required.

Celebrate Milestones and Successes

- **Skydiving Insight:** Skydiving clubs often celebrate first jumps, certifications, and other milestones, which boosts morale and fosters a sense of accomplishment.
- **Workplace Application:** Recognise and celebrate the achievements of new employees whether it's completing their first project or contributing a great idea. This recognition can build confidence and a sense of belonging.

Provide Clear Goals and Expectations

- **Skydiving Insight:** Before a jump skydivers are briefed on what to expect, the process, and the goals for the jump, ensuring everyone understands, is prepared, and is on the same page.
- **Workplace Application:** Clearly communicate job roles, expectations, and objectives to new employees. Understanding their role within the larger team and organisation can help new staff feel more secure and focused.

Encourage Learning and Growth

- **Skydiving Insight:** Skydiving is a learning experience with each jump offering new insights and opportunities for improvement.
- **Workplace Application:** Promote a culture of continuous learning and development. Provide new employees with resources for professional growth and encourage them to pursue opportunities to broaden their knowledge and enhance skills.

Create Safe Spaces for Feedback

- **Skydiving Insight:** After a jump, skydivers often discuss what went well and what could be improved in a constructive and supportive manner.
- **Workplace Application:** Establish regular feedback sessions where new employees can express concerns, ask questions, and offer suggestions. This should be a two-way street, where feedback is given and received openly and constructively.

By incorporating these strategies leaders can create a welcoming and supportive environment for new staff, akin to the camaraderie and inclusivity found in skydiving clubs. Such an approach not only helps in the seamless integration of newcomers but also builds a strong, cohesive team ready to face challenges together.

Back to the jump. The briefing was, as previously mentioned, brief but thorough, a blend of technical details and reassuring guidance. Each weekend we conducted this briefing to ensure it was fresh in our memories, so as we completed it yet again this weekend, we were becoming very familiar with it. For a tandem jump it's really quite simple, and here's how it goes:

- We will strap you to this person who will do everything, period.
- Ensure the strap is around your legs, and nowhere near your 'bits'. You'll find out why when we pull the parachute.
- Hang on and behave yourself.
- Keep your head back, arms in and when you feel a tap on your helmet, extend your arms the way we told you to.
- Don't panic.
- If you panic and put both of us in jeopardy I will punch you in the face and knock your ass out.
- Most importantly, have fun.

As mentioned previously we were given clear expectations, which I fully understood. It's amazing when you face a life and death situation you follow instructions extremely well. And if you don't understand, you ask questions. I asked on which side of the face I could expect the punch. "Let's not ruin the surprise, eh", was the answer, with a little grin that I swear I'll take to my grave with me.

My instructor, a seasoned skydiver with countless jumps to his name, exuded a calm and serious confidence that was both infectious and soothing. He walked me through the process, from the moment we would exit the aircraft to the sensation of freefall, and, finally, the deployment of the parachute. Every step was detailed with precision, leaving no room for doubt or fear, only the excitement of the experience that lay ahead.

Donning the gear felt like a rite of passage. The harness was snug, purposely positioned away from my 'bits', and a constant reminder of the leap I was about to take. As the aircraft ascended, the world below seemed to shrink, a vast patchwork of greens and browns that blurred into the distance. My heart raced, a mix of fear and excitement that made every second feel like an eternity. I was so terrified but I was determined to do it. My friend was also in the plane, a Cessna 206, and he looked as cool as a cucumber. I wondered at that time what that phrase really meant and how stupid it was, and perhaps what a panicked cucumber might look like. Perhaps that's what an aubergine is? And we continued to get higher. I remember thinking that the higher we went, the fear slightly reduced. As the ground became most distant, it no longer felt like a fall I could hurt myself from, like falling from a 20-foot ladder, but rather a beautiful still landscape painting to jump into and become immersed within for the rest of time.

And then, the moment of truth arrived. At 10,000 feet the aircraft door opened, revealing the vast expanse of sky that I was about to embrace. My instructor swung us around so that we faced the door and he inched his way to the edge. He told me to pull my feet right back so my heels touched the underside of the plane. It was only after the jump that I thought, well, I've never been asked to do that before. At this stage, the only part of me touching the plane was my feet as I dangled in a harness, attached to someone who I'm certain had far too much to drink last night (I only know this because I was drinking with him), and who I didn't really know that well, 10,000 feet in the air.

The wind roared in my ears, a fierce reminder of the altitude and the leap that awaited. Just then the engine throttled down and with a nod from my instructor, a tap on the helmet and a deep breath, we jumped. The pilots always glide the aircraft as skydivers are about to jump. I didn't know that and I thought to myself, well maybe this isn't such a bad idea if the plane suddenly just stopped working.

The sensation of freefall was indescribable, a rush of adrenaline that flooded my senses, the world spinning in a whirlwind of colours and sounds. The ground seemed both close and infinitely far away, a distant reality as we plummeted through the sky. My instructor's presence was a constant reassurance, his expertise guiding us through the descent.

And then, with a not so gentle tug, the parachute deployed, and the world suddenly righted itself. The descent slowed, and the serene beauty of the Irish countryside unfolded beneath us. It was a breathtaking spectacle, a panorama of nature's grandeur that stretched to the horizon. The final moments of the descent were peaceful, a stark contrast to the adrenaline-fueled freefall, as we glided gently towards the ground.

The only sound that could be heard was the wind in the parachute and the instructor's voice as he allowed me to steer the parachute. On occasion, whilst still a couple of thousand feet in the air we would practice our landing, which they refer to as a 'flare'. This is when both handles (toggles) are pulled fully down at the same time, capturing as much air in the parachute as possible and basically stopping the forward motion of the parachute to slow the descent for landing. Each time we did this, it removed the sound of the wind in the parachute and the sound of silence was deafening. One of the most wonderful experiences in my life.

Touching down was a moment of triumph, a mix of relief and exhilaration that washed over me. I had done it — I had taken the leap, faced my fear, and emerged with a newfound sense of courage and adventure, excitement and serenity. The experience was transformative, a leap of faith that taught me the true meaning of trust and the thrill of stepping into the unknown.

As I left the Irish Parachute Club that day I carried with me more than just the memory of a skydive. I took with me a sense of accomplishment, a reminder of the day I soared above the earth, embraced the sky, and discovered a strength within I never knew I had.

It was a chapter in my life that I would revisit time and again, a tale of courage, adventure, and the indomitable spirit of the human will to soar beyond the limits of the earth.

It would take a few years until I revisited this experience, as I was determined to do that again, but in the meantime, I discovered, and to the detriment of other friends who had not done it at that time, how to 'pubdive'.

CHAPTER 2

PUBDIVE

The Skydivers' Retreat

I honestly can't remember the origin of the word 'pubdive', but it became a commonly used phrase in the Irish Parachute Club a number of years later when I returned to continue my skydiving adventures. I like to think that I was the one who coined the phrase. I am happy to be contradicted by anyone in the club who believes differently, however my friend and I certainly excelled at using it. We didn't know it at the time, and I think it was certainly later when we reflected on what we were doing that the phrase came into being. But for now I'll take ownership of it and I challenge anyone, these many years later, to refute my claim.

We used to drink in a pub called Dundrum House, in a town called Dundrum (obviously!) in south County Dublin. It was, and still is, a great local pub with a lovely clientele. We grew up in this pub and a lot of major events in our lives took place there. When I say 'we grew up', I mean that we spent a lot of our time in there when we were younger and we got to know a lot of people, some who became friends and some who did not. The next 4 years were quite possibly unbearable for others in our company as all we would speak about was our skydiving experience. I reckon that a larger number of people fell in the 'some who did not' category purely for this reason.

Whoever had the misfortune of sitting with us in the pub and innocently asked the question, "So, anything new?" was subjected to hours of discussion about skydiving and the exhilarating experience we had. I don't even think we cared about who we told about it. I think we just wanted to hear our own voices talking about it.

And the nonsense? Wow! As we tired of our true-life stories, we flawlessly slipped in lies and untruths to embellish the stories so that we could maintain our own enthusiasm to the extent that it became difficult to remember what was real and what was not. Sometimes I wished that we'd done some of the lies because they were honestly more entertaining than the actual truth. There's a great Irish saying that goes, 'Never let the truth get in the way of a good story', however it's important to keep some truth in it.

We had gone rogue. We saw less and less of our friends, and the regulars and staff in the pub began to give us a wide berth. It's funny to think back on it now. The lesson to remember is how people in your network behave when you behave in this manner. Everyone wants to be polite and the ones closest to you will often tell you to 'shut the f&*k up about skydiving', which is often the first warning, and when you don't, they just use their feet. The ones not so close will do their best to maintain relations with you as perhaps they have a benefit to your presence. In this situation, we were great customers of this pub and the owner wanted us to continue coming in, we were probably putting one of his kids through school. But the staff didn't want us there and were sick of our tales, and the other regulars felt the same. In hindsight, I understand why.

Your closest friends can sometimes be the most critical of you, and certainly in my close group of friends, they're not afraid to let me know quite bluntly that I'm being an asshole. And in fairness to them, they have needed to do so many times with me. And sometimes that can be hard to hear. And sometimes it's not something that you want to hear, so there's a tendency to latch onto people who aren't so blunt, and who appear to be more engaging, or perhaps the more appropriate way of phrasing this is, more susceptible to your shit.

Leadership Lesson – Friend or Foe?

This can be obvious when talking to your team and it's natural to latch onto those people. As a leader, there are people who will do their utmost to be noticed by you. They will hang on to every word, they will actively engage with your meetings, sitting up front, making eye contact and generally making you feel so much better about yourself. Some of the time these are just great people who are so enthusiastic about what they do and in such agreement with the direction you are bringing them, but a lot of the time, these people are 'Yes people', previously called 'Yes men/women' (ass-kissers), and whilst it's so comfortable and easy to surround yourself in this world with this type of person, it can also be very detrimental for you.

Leadership Lesson – Image & Exposure vs Performance

A person once told me that there was an equation that explains this behaviour and that equation is:

I + E > P

And what this stands for is,

IMAGE + EXPOSURE > PERFORMANCE

This means that sometimes in business the combination of a certain image or how somebody portrays themselves, and the exposure they receive from the situations they place themselves in and people they meet, can be greater or more powerful than the level of their performance. I am sure you have seen these people, and perhaps a reason for you reading this book is to figure out how to deal with them. The answer is simple. Actually, there are two answers:

1. You can join them.
2. You can run your own race.

But firstly, let's understand a little bit more about these people.

Focusing on image and exposure over performance in the workplace can have both upsides and downsides, affecting not only the individual employee's career trajectory but also the overall culture and efficiency of the organisation.

Here's a breakdown of potential benefits and drawbacks of such behaviour:

Upsides

- **Increased Visibility:**
  Employees who prioritise image and exposure often engage in activities that raise their profile within the organisation. This can lead to increased visibility among peers and supervisors, potentially opening opportunities for advancement and recognition that might not be as readily available to those who solely focus on performance without self-promotion.

- **Networking Opportunities:**
  Prioritising image can lead to better networking opportunities. By positioning themselves as active and engaged members of their professional community, these individuals might gain access to mentors, collaborators, and industry contacts that can offer significant benefits down the line.

- **Leadership Perceptions:**
  Individuals who are adept at managing their image are often perceived as leadership material. Charisma and the ability to effectively com-

municate one's value can be viewed as genuine leadership skills, potentially accelerating career progression.

Downsides

- **Substance vs. Style:**
  A focus on image over performance can lead to a gap between how an individual is perceived and their actual contributions. This discrepancy can result in a lack of trust and respect from colleagues who prioritise substance and may ultimately be detrimental to the individual's reputation and career if their actual performance is consistently subpar.

- **Impact on Team Dynamics:**
  This behaviour can harm team dynamics and morale. When employees notice a coworker succeeding through self-promotion rather than genuine contributions, it can lead to resentment and a decrease in team cohesion. Additionally it might encourage a culture where more employees adopt similar behaviours, leading to a work environment where image is prioritized over actual results.

- **Long-Term Career Impact:**
  While focusing on image might yield short-term gains it can be detrimental in the long run. If an individual's career progression is based more on perception than on real achievements they may find themselves in positions for which they are ill-equipped, leading to potential failure and a negative impact on their long-term career prospects.

- **Organisational Efficiency and Innovation:**
  An organisational culture that rewards image over performance can stifle innovation and efficiency. When the focus shifts away from actual outcomes and towards appearances, it can discourage risk-taking and creativity, which are often necessary for genuine progress and innovation.

In summary, while prioritising image and exposure over performance can offer short-term advantages in terms of visibility and career advancement it carries significant risks that can impact not only the individual's long-term career success but also the overall health and effectiveness of their organisation. Can you imagine if I'd boasted about how great a skydiver I was without actually having had any training at all? (By the way, I did, but that's a later story and most definitely a mistake)? Image vs Substance.

A balance between managing one's image and focusing on substantive contributions is crucial for sustainable career growth and a positive workplace environment.

So, the decision is yours, and I hope that the above upsides and downsides will help you make that decision wisely.

My opinion is that you need to have a blended approach which enhances your profile but is backed by substance. The problem that both my friend and I had whilst we 'pubdived' was that we had no substance. No credibility. We both had 'Skydive' bumper stickers on our cars and we were incredibly proud of them. We often thought, I wonder what the people driving behind us think about us... they must think we're so cool and brave, and exciting and interesting. The truth of it was that nobody cared. The most impact that sticker would have on anyone driving behind was perhaps it would prompt them to book one themselves or serve as a reminder of when they did one themselves. In fact, it was a great advertisement for the club - not us. Never did anyone pull us over to tell us how fabulous we were.

However, there was a time about 2 years after we did our only jump that a person came up to me when I was getting in my car and asked if I was a member of the Irish Parachute Club. I was delighted and felt so special. With such confidence and bravado, I said that I was, to which he replied, 'Are you? I've been a member of the club for the past 3 years and I don't know you'. I felt like such a fraud and was humbled and embarrassed. I tried to back track my answer about being a member, but I couldn't. I had dropped both feet in and there was no escape. I was caught out by a real member of the club. All I had to say was that I once did a tandem skydive and bought the sticker, but I wanted to prove myself to a stranger for some absurd reason, and finally my self-importance and belief that I was something special had caught up on me. How do I get out of this conversation?

I told the truth, and it set me free. Well, there was a little lie wrapped up in it, but it was mostly true. I told him in a much humbler manner that I had done a tandem recently and I had been told by someone there that I became a member for a period of time after that... (that was the lie). He said, 'Oh, good for you, and did you enjoy it?' The conversation continued and it was fantastic. I heard about all his exploits, and the journey he had been on for the past 3 years, and it re-ignited my passion and desire to try it again. He told me that I should try to replicate the feeling of a tandem skydive by doing it myself and told me of the steps and training required to achieve this.

I was back, and God help anyone who had to listen to me for the following 2 years while I prepared for my next jump. I didn't intend for it to take another 2 years, but I really wanted some other friends to experience it with me.

Leadership Lesson – Self-Importance

Sometimes we get caught up in our own self-importance because it can be easier to accept than the reality. Whilst writing this book, I have already imagined it being a bestseller, and have practically written my Pulitzer Prize acceptance speech. Creating the reality is always more difficult than creating a mere perception of it, but a perception is very short lived if you have no substance behind it. How we think others feel about us is sometimes held too high, and we need to learn that this is not as important as how you feel about yourself. And if you're not at the level you wish others to see you at then work harder to get to that level and be comfortable.

I once worked for a financial services company and their Christmas party was organised to take place in a pub in Dublin city. I remember meeting the CEO for a drink in a pub up the road beforehand as we'd agreed to go into the event together. We usually did this before an event and it was always his idea. At the time I thought it was great; I thought that the reason behind it was that he wanted to spend some quality time with me. Well, that was my perception. We had a couple of drinks and as we walked down to this event he said, 'You know, I really enjoy those few drinks we usually have before these things', and as I prepared my response to what I expected him to say next, which was obviously going to be something like, 'it's always good to spend some time with you', or 'I appreciate everything you do for the company and I like to show my appreciation individually with you', he continued to say, 'I just can't stand walking into these events on my own and I know that if I walk in with you the staff will all come to you and leave me alone – you're a great distraction for me'.

I was horrified and so disappointed. We got to the door and the security staff stopped us and asked us where we were going. I said we were joining a group of people from our office for our Christmas party. They said fine and started to let me in, when they asked the CEO the same question, he replied quite abruptly, 'Well it's obviously the same answer because I'm the CEO of the company'. The response from security was immediate and abrupt, 'I couldn't give a shit if you're the Queen of Sheeba, drop the attitude. You're not in your house now Dorothy! Any trouble from you tonight and you'll have me to deal with'.

I guessed the reference to 'Dorothy' was something to do with the Wizard of Oz, but I didn't care. A stranger just took the horror and disappointment that I had just felt and flipped it right back into the CEO's face. He was disgusted. 'Who do they think they're speaking to? How do they not know who I am?'

I just replied, 'Sure, how would they? Not to worry, we're in now', and I thought to myself, maybe it's just as well they don't really know you as they'd never have let you in, and rightly so.

This experience lasted less than 5 minutes from when we left the pub up the road to when we walked into this other venue, but the perception I had about this person had changed tremendously. In leadership, you need to care for your people; it's not possible to hide that because someday your lies will become untangled and the true 'you' will be visible.

I take no joy in letting you know that later that evening one of the staff accidently vomited on the CEO. I take no joy in telling you this as obviously I must have neglected my 'distraction' duties at some stage during the evening. (Well, just a little joy.)

I'll put a pin in the Pulitzer Prize acceptance speech for the moment and move onto the next chapter.

CHAPTER 3

CONVINCING THE CREW

The Challenge of Sky-High Recruitment

At this stage I was hooked. I had spent so much time pubdiving, bluffing my way through conversations and generally setting up a perception of myself that, quite frankly, wasn't true. I needed further substance and validity. It was now about 3 years since I had done the first skydive and I'd been living off that experience over and over again. And it was wearing thin on everyone.

I had slightly drifted apart from the friend who had originally done the jump with me. I had a specific group of friends whom I had grown up with, and this friend was a little older and always a little on the outskirts of that group. He had come into my life after being introduced to me by an old school friend and then drifted back out again. I think he'd found a girlfriend perhaps at this time or another distraction and he didn't seem to be too interested in doing another dive. I really think he definitely preferred the pubdiving aspect, rather than the actual jumping out of a plane aspect but certainly didn't want to admit that.

A couple of years later whilst myself and the crew I had assembled were back in the Irish Parachute Club, he had travelled to New Zealand and supposedly did another one. There was never any evidence provided of this other than his personal account of it. Supposedly he had done a 'solo' freefall, which every diver knows wouldn't be possible unless you followed a specific training program (which I'll be talking about in later chapters), however when he returned from New Zealand, the stories of bravery and courage were both captivating and exhilarating and totally bullshit. This guy was an excellent pubdiver and I don't think I ever gave him the credit that he deserved for that.

I really didn't want to go back to the Club on my own; I really wanted to continue my journey of learning to skydive. I'm not sure why I didn't have the courage to do it on my own. Perhaps I was slightly scared of the overpowering people who were there or perhaps I thought that if I didn't have people around me spurring me on I might not achieve my goal. Perhaps I was worried about Billy Murphy and whether he would remember me - and his soiled bed. I told you that my friend had vomited in one of Billy's beds, but, it was actually me who did it. We had both shared a twin room, and whilst we both had a lot of drink the night before I made it down for breakfast and my friend had not. Billy had asked, 'Is your friend coming for breakfast?' and I replied that he wasn't feeling great, so probably not. He wasn't feeling great because he still had all of that alcohol in his stomach whereas mine was empty. When he got up and saw the vomit he assumed it was his because he felt so bad and I felt so good. We really weren't the smartest people back then. Anyway, we also assumed that Billy would believe it was him, so I felt no need to confuse things further by telling him it was me. Anyway I assume when he picks up this book for the first time he won't expect to read anything surprising about his involvement in the events that occurred, but there you go... life is full of surprises.

SURPRISE!!

I needed to go back to my group of friends and convince them to try it for themselves. I had bored the pants off them for the past 3 years and I really couldn't see any of them buying into my dream. The last time I'd mentioned skydiving to this most sacred and inner circle of friends the response was an abrupt, 'Would you please just shut the hell up about skydiving?' I knew it was gonna be a tough sell to this crowd.

Leadership Lesson – The First Follower

Sometimes in leadership it can be tough to convince people to join you on your journey, but a lot of the time all you need is one and then others follow. There are many discussions about the importance of the 'first follower' and Derek Sivers' TED Talk titled "How to Start a Movement" humorously and effectively demonstrates this concept using a video of a dancing man at a music festival. Initially dancing alone, he seems eccentric. When the first follower joins him they together create a sense of legitimacy and fun, quickly attracting more people until a critical mass forms, turning the initial act into a widespread movement.

The concept of the "first follower" is crucial in leadership theory, highlighting the role of the initial supporter who joins a leader in a new initiative. This person is pivotal for several reasons, fundamentally changing the dynamics of leadership and influence.

Here's why the first follower is so important in leadership:

- **Validation of the Leader's Vision:**
  The first follower acts as a crucial validator of the leader's ideas and vision. By choosing to follow they lend credibility to the leader's actions or proposals, signalling to others that the vision or idea is worth

considering. This validation is essential in the early stages of any initiative when scepticism or indifference might be high.

- **Transformation from Lone Actor to Leader:**
  The act of the first follower transforms the leader from a lone actor into someone with a following. This is a critical juncture in the development of leadership as leadership inherently requires followers. Without at least one follower, a person's leadership is theoretical at best.

- **Encouraging Others to Follow:**
  Sometimes in groups it can be difficult to be the first one. The first follower lowers the barrier for others to join. They serve as a bridge between the leader and the rest of the potential followers, demonstrating that it's safe and valuable to follow. This can create a snowball effect, where more and more people feel comfortable joining, significantly amplifying the leader's impact.

- **Demonstrating How to Follow:**
  The first follower also teaches others how to follow the leader's vision. Their actions provide a template or model for others to emulate, showing that following is not just about accepting the leader's ideas but actively supporting and contributing to them.

- **Enhancing the Leader's Ideas:**
  First followers often play a critical role in shaping and refining the leader's vision. They can provide feedback, suggest improvements, and offer insights that the leader may not have considered. This collaboration can make the initial idea stronger and more resilient.

- **Risk-taking and Courage:**
  The first follower takes a significant risk by stepping out and supporting a new idea or vision. Their courage can inspire others to take risks

as well, fostering an environment where innovation and bold moves are encouraged.

- **Social Proof and Momentum Building:**
  In social psychology the concept of social proof suggests that people are more likely to engage in an action if they see others doing it. The first follower serves as social proof, indicating to others that following is a desirable action. This can build momentum for the leader's vision or initiative.

The importance of the first follower in leadership underscores that leadership is not a solo endeavour; it's a communal process that relies on the interaction between the leader, the first follower, and subsequent followers. The dynamics between these roles can determine the success or failure of a movement, initiative, or idea.

Sometimes the best first follower is that person in a company or group of friends who is the most outspoken. And sometimes that person is more negative than others, but this is the person that can either bring success or ultimately failure to your vision. Think carefully about who you choose, but avoiding the person who was just described could be extremely detrimental to your dreams.

Ensuring that the most outspoken and sometimes negative person in a team or group of friends becomes the first follower can be a strategic move for several reasons, particularly in the context of leadership and change management. This approach can leverage the influence and perspective of a critical team member to facilitate broader acceptance and support for an initiative. And although this person may be the most outspoken, ensure that they are liked, trusted, and accepted by the team or no one will follow.

Here are key reasons why this strategy can be important:

- **Turning Scepticism into Advocacy:**
  Outspoken and critical team members often command attention and can influence the opinions of others. If you can convince them of the value of a new idea or change their transition from scepticism to advocacy can be particularly powerful. Their support can lend significant credibility to the initiative, as their endorsement implies a thorough critique and subsequent approval.

- **Utilizing Their Influence:**
  Outspoken individuals usually have strong influence within a team. Their endorsement can lead to a domino effect, encouraging others who respect their opinion to also support the initiative. This can be crucial in overcoming resistance and building momentum.

- **Enhancing the Initiative with Critical Feedback:**
  One reason outspoken team members may initially resist new ideas is their ability to identify potential flaws or challenges that others might overlook. By engaging them early and addressing their concerns you can refine and strengthen the initiative, ensuring that it is more robust and likely to succeed.

- **Demonstrating Leadership Openness and Confidence:**
  By actively engaging with the most critical voices and working to convert them into supporters a leader demonstrates confidence in the value of the initiative as well as openness to feedback. This can enhance the leader's credibility and the team's trust in leadership, showing that all voices are valued and considered.

- **Building a Stronger Team Dynamic:**
  Successfully converting a critical voice into a first follower can improve team dynamics. It shows the team that respectful dissent is not only

tolerated but is a valued part of the process. This can encourage a more open, trusting, and collaborative team environment, where members feel empowered to share diverse viewpoints.

- **Creating a More Resilient Change Process:**
  Engaging with and converting critics early in the change process can help anticipate objections and resistance, allowing for strategies to address these issues proactively. This can make the implementation of new ideas smoother and more resilient to challenges.

- **Facilitating Comprehensive Adoption:**
  When the most critical voices within a team become supporters, it signals to the entire organisation that the initiative has been rigorously examined and deemed valuable. This comprehensive shift can facilitate deeper and more widespread adoption of the change.

However it's important to approach this strategy with sensitivity and understanding. The goal is not to suppress dissent or force agreement but to genuinely engage with and address the concerns of critical team members. By doing so leaders can harness the potential of their most outspoken members to foster a more inclusive, committed, and effective team.

So I needed to find my first follower, and here were the contenders:

Sean. Sean and I first met when we were 7 years of age, in 1977. Sean lived up the road from me and he was exactly one week younger. He gate-crashed my 7th birthday party and brought a teddy bear, which was missing one eye, as a present. It was also a little bit dirty and a 'lot' bit smelly. At that time, parents were always looking for opportunities to put their children out of the house for a much time as possible, so his parents had seen balloons outside of my house that morning and they decided to take a chance, not knowing the age, or sex, of the child whose birthday it was. In their eyes, it was worth the risk. 'Sometimes you've just got to get the little fecker out from under our feet'.

Sean and I hit it off and a lifetime friendship ensued. A week later I was cordially invited to his birthday party, and I brought him back the teddy bear, this time fully blind and significantly smellier.

Over the course of our friendship we got into a lot of mischief. We were quite possibly the most immature and irresponsible people you could meet. It didn't matter what other people said about the stupid things we did. Once we both agreed that they were all wrong, and that our idea wasn't a stupid idea, we did it. I won't go into detail about the things we did, and in fairness to both of us, some of them were legal, but this is exactly why Sean wasn't my guy. If Sean was the first to start dancing on a mountain top, like in the 'First Follower' video (I hope you've watched already), not only would people not join him, they'd leave believing that he wasn't dancing but jumping up and down to cause a landslide. Sean was out... and later in this book you'll probably agree that that was a wise choice.

Declan. Declan and I first met when we were about 13 years old. He is 3 months younger than I am, and he lived about 2 streets away from where I lived. He would have definitely brought me a filthy teddy bear if he had known me when I was 7, in fact he's brought me many other filthy items in the time that I've known him, so a teddy bear would have been a drop in the ocean for this man. I met Declan because he lived on the street of a scout leader who myself and another friend had befriended back then. We used to visit this scout leader's house on occasion, and Declan, amongst a few others, used to hang around on the street. We were all around the same age so we got on famously. I used to take this scout leader's dog for a walk in the local park and that's how I met Declan and the others. They were a great bunch of people.

Some things happened at that time with the scout leader which I won't go into, and whilst I wasn't directly and physically affected, others were significantly hurt. And in hindsight, I was, too, but in different ways. In fact, nearly 30 years later, when the Gardai knocked on my door, asked me if I knew this scout leader, and mentioned his name, I said, 'You know, I'd always wondered if this day would come'. There were suspicions back then, but nothing more. For clarity, Declan was not the other friend who had befriended this person with me and was not impacted in this manner in any way. He did however on many occasions offer his suspicions, which I disregarded, and which I now heavily regret.

Declan spent a lot of his years directly after school travelling and 'chasing a dragon'. I used to tell him that dragons didn't exist, but he always said I wouldn't understand. I still don't. Some of his decision making at the time was a little scary, and sometimes there was a look in his eye that would genuinely concern me... and sometimes there still is. But he was busy, and at this time we didn't see a lot of him, so I didn't think he was my guy. A great guy, but not my 'first follower'.

Conor. Conor and I first met when I was about 13 years old and at the same time that I met Declan who was the same age. Conor was a little younger than us, and at 13 years old, a couple of years younger was massive. I had befriended his brother as they lived next door to Declan, and his brother was one of the group who used to hang out on the street with Declan. After a couple of years, Conor became more prominent in my life and his brother slipped away into different interests. Conor was and still is a very faith orientated and spiritual person. A lovely fella and a great friend. Whilst I was going on about skydiving, or pubdiving, Conor never succumbed and was much more comfortable keeping his feet firmly on the ground. I didn't think many people would listen to Conor because he was very clear that he wasn't going to do it. He wasn't the guy, however I mention him because he was instrumental in introducing me to a number of the people who did and the very person who became 'my guy'!

Liam. Liam is Conor's cousin and although I don't remember exactly how old I was when I met him, it feels like he's been around since I met Conor and his brother. Perhaps it may have been a year or two later. At the very start and for quite a number of years, neither of us really understood each other. Liam was not pleased about how Sean and I used to behave and wouldn't be subtle about telling us. The manner in which he approached us wasn't suitable for a positive reaction from either of us, and it always felt as though he was scolding us, which made us want to rebel even further. He always spoke a lot of sense, but the manner was far too mature, and despite being a number of years younger than both of us biologically, he was miles older than us mentally. To be honest I never thought he'd take such as risk, so I discounted him pretty quickly, and I thought that if there was ever going to be someone who would put all of their effect trying to stop all of their friends jumping out of perfectly good airplanes, it would have been him.

I was wrong. He did jump with us, and I think he'd agree with me when I say there was nothing 'perfectly good' about these airplanes back then. But still, he wasn't the guy!!

Kieran. Kieran and I first met when we were about 18 years old. He's the oldest of our group of friends, being 3 months older than Sean and me. And he has always acted his age, something I certainly never did. He lived 2 doors down the road from Jack, who I'll mention shortly. He and Jack grew up together as neighbours and were always as thick as thieves. Kieran is extremely intelligent and exceptionally sensible. He is the guy in the group who was always sensible with money, and inadvertently was always the guy we all borrowed money from. He was the first person I know to open a Credit Union account and would often be referred to as someone who wouldn't 'spend Christmas'. He was, and still is, very frugal. He and Liam were the people amongst us who spoke the most sense. Neither of them provided us with the most exciting words to hear when we were younger, and many others in the group were faster, and wittier, and funnier, but these guys really kept us grounded, or, well, tried their best to. Kieran was also what we referred to as a 'machine'. Whatever this guy did, he did it 100%, and he told us about 120%. A little bit of me thought that if Kieran joined us on this skydiving adventure that he'd never stop, and that kind of scared me a little. How true that ended up being. More on that later.

A long time ago, I tried stand-up comedy for the first time which eventually turned into a part-time hobby for nearly 25 years. The very first time I had been allowed on stage in a comedy club in Dublin, I asked Kieran to come with me. I wanted someone to be there to give me moral support and to be able to talk to about it afterwards. I picked Kieran because I really thought that I was going to be dreadful, and I feared that if I failed so badly, Kieran would be the most kind in his commentary when explaining the disaster to the rest of the group. That's the kind of guy Kieran is but sometimes his views or comments weren't scathing enough, or funny enough for people to pay attention to, so he wasn't my 'first follower' guy!! However, I'll never forget the support he gave me that night.

Aidan. Aidan and I met around the same time as I met Kieran and Jack. Both Aidan and Jack went to school with Conor, and as I began to know Conor I also came to know Aidan and Jack. Aidan is honestly one of the nuttiest people I know and also one of the smoothest. Always dressed in the best clothes, Aidan and his family lived in a big house in the Dublin mountains, not too far from where we grew up. He was far to suave to be my guy and the undercurrent of nuttiness probably made my decision for me. Due to the things that Aidan had previously done I didn't think many would follow him. After a heavy night drinking while he was in college, rather than attempting to go home, he slept in a tree across the road from college and was still late for class the next morning. One Christmas he got mugged by Santa. He left a house party in the middle of the night on a cold, snowy night and only made it as far as the field across the road where he fell asleep. He woke up later that morning without his coat, wallet, and shoes. We all thought that Santa must have been extra cold that year. One occasion I'll never forget was at a party in his parent's house in the Dublin mountains. After a significant volume of alcohol, Aidan fell asleep in the bath. A number of us thought it would be funny to turn on the taps, and he only awoke when the bath was half full. As we were laughing and he was trying to establish what was going on, he also began to laugh. We thought it was astonishing that he took this joke in such good form, until he said, 'Do you all think I just jumped into this cold bath before I went to sleep? No, because that would have been stupid; I firstly lined the bottom of it with all of your coats'. And that's exactly what he did and we all had to walk home that night in the freezing cold with cold wet coats. He wasn't my guy!!

Jack. Jack and I met through Conor when I was about 18 years old and he was 16 years old. Jack was the one person who consistently gave out to Sean and me. I don't think he believed that he could change Sean, and in hindsight, he was right... it was a woman who did that for Sean and a fine job she did of it, and in my opinion, just in the nick of time. But Jack never gave up on me. As much as Jack would protest his disgust on our behaviour, he did it in an empathetic manner and without making us feel bad. I was very disappointed in myself every time Jack would speak to me, however most of the time I didn't do anything to change. Jack was a straight talker and still is, but with a certain non-confrontational edge to it. He came from a place of caring, and whether he actually cared or not, it felt to me like it did. Jack is the glue that binds all of our group together, although he may not believe so. If it weren't for him keeping in touch with everyone individually throughout the year, I really don't think many of us would see each other very much. Although I may have not listened to what he was saying to me, I certainly did hear his concerns, and over time I fully came to believe that it was his influence that turned the corner for me. A good guy, with no malice, and someone who everyone listened to and respected. And it's the same to this day. I had found my guy! My 'first follower' was Jack!!

I was back and the dream was alive, and soon, if the persuading was successful, I would return to the Irish Parachute Club with some of my closest friends and continue my journey. I was delighted, and scared shitless, yet again!!

Leadership Lesson – Building the Team to Achieve the Dream

As a leader convincing your crew, or team, to embark on a challenging endeavour such as skydiving, mirrors essential leadership qualities and skills crucial for success in various contexts, from corporate environments to adventurous pursuits. Here are six reasons why this ability is important:

- **Vision Sharing and Alignment:**
  Leaders must articulate a clear and compelling vision that motivates and inspires their team. Convincing the crew to participate in a skydive reflects the leader's ability to share a vision (the exhilarating experience and accomplishment of skydiving) in a way that aligns with the team members' personal goals or interests.
- **Building Trust and Confidence:**
  Convincing others to step out of their comfort zone, especially for an activity that involves risk like skydiving, requires a high level of trust. Leaders need to establish trust not only in their judgment but also in

the safety and value of the experience, thereby strengthening the team's confidence in their leadership and in each other.

- **Enhancing Team Cohesion and Morale:**
  Undertaking a challenging activity together, which doesn't need to be skydiving, can strengthen team bonds, improve morale, and foster a sense of unity. The shared experience of overcoming fears and achieving a goal can translate into stronger teamwork and collaboration in professional settings.

- **Developing Resilience and Adaptability:**
  By pushing team members to confront fears and uncertainties, leaders encourage personal and group resilience. These experiences teach teams to adapt to unforeseen challenges, a skill that is invaluable in navigating the complexities of business and life.

- **Cultivating Leadership in Others:**
  Leaders who encourage their teams to undertake challenges are also fostering leadership qualities within their team members. Such experiences allow individuals to demonstrate courage, take initiative, and support one another, cultivating a culture of leadership throughout the organisation.

- **Achieving Personal and Professional Growth:**
  Convincing the group to engage in a skydive is not just about the physical act itself but about encouraging personal growth, pushing boundaries, and expanding comfort zones. These experiences can translate into professional environments, encouraging creativity, innovation, and a willingness to tackle difficult tasks or projects.

In essence the ability to convince the group to take on challenging endeavours like skydiving showcases a leader's ability to inspire, unite, and develop their team, qualities that are pivotal for success in any leadership role.

Once Jack was on board the persuasion was easy. Within a couple of weeks a few of us had agreed to go to the Irish Parachute Club. For me it would be another tandem skydive, and for them, their first.

And wow, the story has only just begun now!!

CHAPTER 4

IN FREE FALL TOGETHER

Building Your Ideal Team for Business Success

Leadership Lesson – Surrounding Yourself with the Right People

Having the right people around you when undertaking something challenging is crucial for numerous reasons, impacting not only the success of the endeavour itself but also your personal growth, resilience, and the quality of the experience. I needed the right people to support me, keep me on track, and most importantly to have fun with along the way.

Here are some key reasons why the company you keep in challenging times is so important:

- **Support and Encouragement:**
  Facing challenges can be daunting and there will inevitably be moments of doubt or the desire to give up. The right people provide emotional support, encouragement, and motivation to keep going, especially when things get tough. Their belief in your abilities can bolster your confidence and determination.

- **Diverse Perspectives and Skills:**
Challenges often require solutions that are not immediately apparent or that require skills that you may not possess. Having a diverse group around you means access to a variety of perspectives and skills, which can be crucial for overcoming obstacles and finding innovative solutions.

- **Shared Effort and Responsibility:**
Tackling a challenge with the right team allows for the distribution of effort and responsibility. This not only makes the task more manageable but also creates a sense of shared purpose and collaboration, enhancing the likelihood of success.

- **Accountability:**
People who understand your goals and the challenges you face can hold you accountable for your actions and decisions. This accountability can be a powerful motivator, keeping you focused and on track towards achieving your objectives.

- **Learning and Growth:**
Being surrounded by the right people in challenging situations can significantly accelerate your learning and personal growth. You can learn from their experiences, insights, and approaches to problem-solving, which can be invaluable in developing your own skills and resilience.

- **Risk Mitigation:**
The right team can help identify potential risks and develop strategies to mitigate them. Their collective experience, insight, and wisdom can be crucial in foreseeing possible pitfalls and planning accordingly, reducing the likelihood of failure.

- **Moral and Ethical Guidance:**
When faced with difficult decisions, having trusted individuals around you can provide the moral and ethical guidance necessary to navigate

complex situations. Their input can help ensure that your choices align with your values and the greater good.

- **Emotional Resilience:**
  The emotional toll of facing challenges can be significant. The right people can help you manage stress, anxiety, and fear, providing a buffer against the psychological strain of challenging endeavours.

- **Celebrating Success:**
  When you overcome a challenge celebrating with those who have supported and worked alongside you can be incredibly rewarding. These moments of shared joy and accomplishment can strengthen bonds and make the success even more meaningful.

- **Safety Net:**
  In case of failure or setbacks having the right people around you acts as a safety net, offering practical help, advice on what to do next, and emotional support to help you cope with disappointment.

In summary, the right companions in challenging times can make the difference between success and failure, growth and stagnation. They provide not just the skills and support needed to overcome obstacles, but also enrich the journey, making it a more rewarding and transformative experience.

Sometimes these days the larger an organisation the more difficult it is to get the right person into the right role. There are so many hoops to jump through, and effectively what larger organisations have done is reversed the psychology of the hiring process. Forgive the upcoming rant, but here it is...

Leadership Lesson – Don't Always Rely on other Departments

As discussed above, it's so important to have the right people around you, whether it's in your personal, or professional life. HR departments these days place a lot of their concentration on ensuring that the companies they work for are not sued by their employees, which of course does happen and can be very detrimental for a business. However sometimes these preventive measures can also be detrimental to a business.

In my opinion it's true purpose and value has sadly become lost over the past few years. And don't blame our HR colleagues because all of us are to blame.

What it should be:

HR's core function should be as a key strategic partner to the management of an organisation. Their input should help support and strengthen the business by identifying the right people for the right roles in a proactive manner, ensuring that those people are capable of performing said role, and helping those who need help. And in a nutshell... that's it!!

What it shouldn't be:

A reactive Employment Law advisory service to prevent a business from being sued by their own staff.

To be clear, I'm not a fan of the new HR but I understand why it's ended up this way. I'm also not an HR person. I'm an Ops person and recognise the value of a well-functioning HR team doing what they should be doing.

If you recognise your HR team in the 2nd description and you're frustrated with them 'always bringing problems' to the table and 'getting in the way of productivity', your problem is not with them... your problem is far deeper within the business and HR is just the messenger.

Don't shoot the messenger... listen... they're usually a lot closer to the action. Empower and trust them to help you put the right people into the right roles wherever that role sits in the company structure.

'If you've hired people to protect you from being sued, perhaps stop giving people a reason to do so'.

Generally, the reason why businesses are being sued by their employees is management, and no matter how good your HR team is, they are effectively emptying the water out of the boat without repairing the holes. The holes are where the attention needs to be placed, but unfortunately a lot of businesses react to problems, rather than proactively identifying potential issues and plugging the 'holes' before these issues become problems.

The HR departments spends so much time writing and implementing policies and procedures, while management finds ways to circumvent them. This is where most of the legal cases come from. I challenge you to research past workplace relations legal cases and find one where the company strictly abided by their policies and procedures and lost the case. They are few and far between. Seriously, take my word for it: listen to the message and stop wasting your precious time searching through legal case files just to try to prove me wrong.

The point is that a lot of managers don't even know their own company policies and procedures. And sometimes I don't blame them as they can be very drawn out and boring to read. But they are so important and will always be thrown at you in court should the unfortunate day come. Here's a tip for you which worked very well for me in a previous life. Introduce a Policy & Procedures section in your weekly meetings and invite HR to attend. It doesn't have to take much time, so just pick one each week and bring everyone through it. If you are using slides, include the bullet points in the slides (sometimes HR will do the slides for you if you ask nicely) and circulate to everyone after the meeting. This has a number of positive effects:

1. It teaches you the company policies and procedures.
2. It teaches your team the company policies and procedures.
3. It shows your team and your management that you care about the company policies and procedures.
4. And most importantly, it provides you and the company with protection, and here's why:

Most companies have very long employee handbooks and policy documents. Employees are provided with a copy of these when they join and they sign to say that they've read and understood them. And despite being paid while they read these documents, they generally don't. Did you? Probably not either. If you are ever in a position in court where you say that the employee read and understood these documents when they joined the company, quite often years previously, and expect that the court will accept this testimony of 'employee understanding' without any evidence of refresher training, you are sadly mistaken. On one occasion a client of mine attempted this defence, obviously against my advice, and the employee's solicitor presented my client with their own employee handbook and asked them what was on page 39. Obviously, my client didn't know the answer and the solicitor was able to state that if the owner of the business didn't know what was on that page, how could they expect their employees to know. Now obviously that's a little severe, but the judge agreed, and the employee won their case with the defence of not knowing or understanding the policies that the company used to dismiss them. There were a lot of other issues that the company's management was guilty of in this case, however the point of the policies is still valid.

If you are doing refresher courses every week in your team meetings your employees will find it very difficult to use that defence, which will protect the company, and once you are abiding by these policies when dealing with your team, you are protecting yourself. Once this state of utopia is achieved your HR Department can return to identifying good people to place in the correct positions to strengthen the structure of your business.

Let's work together to ensure that your HR department is spending time effectively and efficiently and helping you to build a strong and sustainable business, not just putting out fires. It can be a vicious cycle to get caught in, but change happens one step at a time, so why not take the first step. The alternatives are too costly to consider, and if your HR Department continues to place an overemphasis on this aspect, it can inadvertently lead to several detrimental effects on the business, such as:

- **Eroding Trust:**
  When employees perceive HR as solely focused on protecting the company's interests it can erode trust between the workforce and HR. Employees may feel that their concerns and well-being are secondary to the company's legal protection, leading to a decline in morale and engagement.

- **Suppressing Voices:**
  A primary focus on avoiding litigation can result in a culture where employees are hesitant to voice concerns, report issues, or provide feedback for fear of retaliation, being disregarded, or worse – being labelled a troublemaker. This suppression of voices can prevent the organisation from identifying and addressing problems early, potentially leading to bigger issues down the line.

- **Neglecting Employee Development and Satisfaction:**
  Resources and attention may be diverted from initiatives aimed at employee development, satisfaction, and engagement towards litigation

avoidance strategies. This shift in focus can result in a lack of growth opportunities, decreased job satisfaction, and higher turnover rates.

- **Impacting Company Culture:**
  A litigious-focused approach can contribute to a defensive, cautious company culture, stifling innovation, and risk-taking. Companies may become too rigid in their policies and procedures, making them less adaptable to change and potentially hindering their competitive edge.

- **Creating a Compliance-Only Mindset:**
  While compliance with laws and regulations is crucial, an overemphasis can lead to a compliance-only mindset, where ticking boxes becomes more important than the spirit of these laws — namely, to create a fair, inclusive, and respectful workplace. This approach might overlook the importance of building a positive workplace culture beyond just avoiding legal pitfalls.

- **Resource Drain:**
  Over-focusing on legal protection can lead to significant allocation of time, money, and resources towards defensive strategies and legal consultations. These resources might be better utilised in proactive workforce development, innovation, and strategic initiatives that contribute directly to the business's growth and sustainability.

Balancing the need to protect the organisation legally with fostering a positive, inclusive, and engaging work environment is crucial. HR departments should aim to protect the company while also advocating for and supporting employees, ensuring their concerns are heard and addressed, and promoting a culture of trust and mutual respect. This balanced approach not only mitigates legal risks but also contributes to a healthier, more productive, and more innovative organisation.

Remember the time when you worked for a small company, or in fact had your own small company? And remember how important it was to you to ensure the right people were doing the right jobs, and your people were treated fairly and respectfully because that was your way of doing things? When a company grows and more people join, achieving this goal can be more difficult, so it's important to remember the fundamentals: ensure your team members know the rules, ensure you do, too, ensure your team understands what is expected from them, and each member understands their role, and ensure lines of clear communication. These are the fundamentals of every basic human relationship. And now that you have recruited the right person into the right role, your relationship with that person begins. And it is up to you to ensure that this relationship grows and blossoms... or your back to square one again.

So with the help of Jack and his influencing style, which was something like, 'I'm doing it, so if I can so can you', I had my team for our skydiving adventure, and each of them provided me with a different skillset I believed I would need to help me achieve my goal, which was to successfully replicate the experience of a tandem skydive from 10,000 feet, without the burden of some lunatic strapped to my back. There was a long way to go, and a lot of exciting new experiences ahead of me and the lads, but one step at a time... next stop, The Irish Parachute Club in Clonbullogue, Offaly in 1998, with a new drive and a new team.

Can't wait!!

CHAPTER 5

LEAPING INTO THE UNKNOWN

The First Steps of Skydiving Training

Learning to skydive on your own is one hell of an experience. There are so many factors to consider and so many aspects to prepare for. Take my word for it; when you see skydivers on the TV, they really do make it look easy, but as with anything in life, the more practice, the more perfect. Now, there's another way of looking at the phrase, "practice makes perfect". This is a phrase we've all grown up with, however someone said to me recently that a more accurate phrase should be "practice makes permanent", which really made me think.

Think of it like this; while you need to practice to improve, you need to ensure you're practicing correctly, otherwise you're making those mistakes a permanent feature and therefore so much harder to fix. We practice correctly for our driving test, and once we pass that test, we start bringing in bad habits. As we continue to practice those bad habits every time we drive, over time they become permanent. So be careful when you say, "practice makes perfect", because all it really does is make what you practice "permanent".

This sport is a serious business, and every aspect of this business needs to be treated with the respect it deserves. There are rules that are in place to be followed. These are not just guidelines or suggestions for you to decide which have merit and which don't. These are rules which cannot under any circumstance be broken. And everyone abides by them. The skydiving community is full of the craziest, most fun-loving, exciting, and somewhat non-compliant people you can imagine. People from every walk of life; from Army Rangers to bus drivers, from police officers to office workers, and they all have one thing in common: they all want to live to see tomorrow, therefore they all follow the rules. And if you don't, you don't get to jump. It's as simple as that.

There are no HR procedures to follow to dismiss someone from the club. There's no time for that and it's too dangerous to allow for a 'presumed innocent until proven guilty' approach. They have a simple yet effective process in place which involves the use of the 'black card'. These cards are instantly given to anyone who does something incredibly stupid or unsafe and whilst in possession of this black card, they are not permitted to jump until an investigation is completed, which often only confirms the decision. The CCI, or Chief Club Instructor, would issue these cards. Somebody who decides to not follow the rules could cause the death of themselves and someone else. In effect this is an instant suspension pending investigation.

As mentioned in a previous chapter, when doing a tandem skydive, due to the hazardous nature of this activity, the instructor is fully prepared to take whatever action required to prevent you from doing something that will put both of you in danger. Someone once said that they'd have no hesitation in punching you in the face to knock you out if that was the only way to calm you down and mitigate the risk. I never saw that happen, never experienced it and never heard of it happening to anyone in the club, however I was always comfortable knowing that they were prepared to do everything in their power to keep me safe, whether the method was deemed appropriate or not.

I recently spoke to a lifeguard and their remit is sometimes the same. If they are trying to save your life and you are in such a panic that you are pulling both of you under the water, they will take drastic action, without a second's thought, to disable you so you can't fight against what they're trying to do: save your life. And this is exactly what we would expect them to do whilst they are trying to save our lives. This person also told me that one of those strategies is to let you drown just a little more, if required; for example, they would pull back a little, and more or less wait until the person was in so much trouble that they became unconscious - harsh as this approach may seem, sometimes trying anything else places both the person being rescued, and the rescuer in more danger than necessary. However, highlighting this strategy probably wouldn't do a lot for the reputation of lifeguards - some things we're just better off not knowing about.

They won't write you a letter to invite you to a meeting to discuss your behaviour; or prolong the inevitable; you're just out and that's it. Your safety and the safety of the others around you is the top priority for the management of the club, and they do not allow exhaustive processes and procedures to delay the removal of a safety risk. I've been told that a follow up letter may be issued with the reasons for why you are no longer welcome at the club. I would expect nothing less from a professional who is trying to keep me alive.

We don't know how we will handle extreme events until we experience them, and the mistakes we could make under that sort of pressure could be fatal, therefore having someone close to you who is prepared and willing to take drastic action is so important for you (and them), because in the end, you want to live to see tomorrow.

Although when you go for a pleasant swim in the sea or local swimming pool there are no warning signs that say, 'If you don't behave, we reserve the right to punch your lights out', but the unspoken rules remain in place from the viewpoint of the lifeguard.

In skydiving, you are told this from the very beginning. The expectations of you, the rules that you must abide to, and the consequences of breaking those rules are fully explained to you from the very start. And if you're not happy with them, you know where the door is – it's that simple.

Leadership Lesson – Setting Expectations

The similarities between this kind of organisation and the one that you work in are striking, however they are not treated with the same respect. Why? Because in business your livelihood may be on the line but your life is not. And no one gets to punch you in the face.

It is so important in business to ensure as a leader that you set the expectations with your team, and you follow through on any infractions, abiding by the processes and procedures your organisation has in place. As strange as it may seem it is easier to have a healthy, respectful and fun environment for your team to work in if you deliver your style of leadership in a 'flexible, but with strict rules' manner. And the more that people abide by the rules, the more fun you can have. As people stray away from the rules, these behaviours start to eat into your time, meaning that you can no longer spend as much quality time with your team, enjoying the work together and supporting those who need your support. Instead you are distracted by poor behaviour and caught up in endless meetings, and so on and so on.

Although sometimes it's easier to shy away from confrontation and maybe turn a blind eye, unless you proactively manage and deal with the slightest infringements, you will end up having to reactively deal with a lot worse than that.

You owe it to yourself and to your team to take action immediately. If you don't, your team, and not just the ones who have decided to behave inappropriately, will rightly believe that your style of leadership is purely 'flexible', without the strict rules part, and then your troubles will begin. Never assume that people *won't* abide by the rules. The majority will and are happy to do so but there will inevitably be those who won't.

Just as we signed up to the rules of the Irish Parachute Club and understood the consequences, so do the majority of people when they start a job. We did it because we wanted to jump out of planes... they do it because they want to work, create, and keep their jobs. If these expectations aren't clearly delivered and understood at the very start, then they may as well not exist.

Comparing the importance of abiding by the rules in the professional environment and in the world of skydiving reveals both similarities and differences in terms of safety, success, and ethical conduct.

Leadership Lesson – Adherence to Rules

Here's a breakdown of how adherence to rules matters in both contexts:

In the Professional Environment

- **Safety and Well-being:**
  In certain professions, especially those involving physical labour, healthcare, food services, and manufacturing, rules and regulations are critical to ensuring the safety and well-being of employees. While not as immediately life-threatening as skydiving, the consequences of ignoring safety protocols can lead to serious injuries or even fatalities.

- **Quality and Standards:**
  Adherence to rules ensures that products, services, and operations meet established quality standards. This is crucial for maintaining a company's reputation, ensuring customer satisfaction, and avoiding legal issues.

- **Ethical Conduct:**
  In the professional environment, rules often encompass ethical guidelines that prevent corruption, ensure fair treatment of employees and customers, and protect the company's integrity. This includes adhering to laws, respecting confidentiality, and avoiding conflicts of interest.

- **Efficiency and Productivity:**
  Rules and protocols in a professional setting help streamline processes, ensuring that operations run smoothly and efficiently. This organisational structure is vital for brand consistency, meeting deadlines, achieving targets, and sustaining profitability.

In the World of Skydiving

- **Safety and Survival:**
  In skydiving following rules is not just important — it's a matter of life and death. Adhering to safety protocols, such as checking equipment properly, understanding weather conditions, and following jump procedures, is crucial to prevent accidents and fatalities.

- **Skill Development:**
  Rules and guidelines in skydiving also ensure that individuals progress through levels of difficulty safely. They are designed to ensure that skydivers have the necessary skills and experience before attempting more challenging jumps.

- **Respect for Authority and Environment:**
  Following rules in skydiving shows respect for the authorities regulating the sport, including instructors and safety officers. It also involves

respecting the environment and the airspace, ensuring that the sport does not negatively impact others.

- **Community and Trust:**
  Adherence to rules fosters a sense of community and trust among skydivers. Knowing that everyone is following the same safety standards creates an environment where individuals can rely on one another, enhancing the overall experience.

While the immediate consequences of not following rules may vary — ranging from professional repercussions to life-threatening situations — the underlying importance of rule adherence is fundamental in both domains. In the professional environment it ensures safety, quality, ethical behaviour, and efficiency. In skydiving it is absolutely critical for safety, skill progression, respect, and community trust.

The level of risk involved in skydiving elevates the importance of rule adherence to a matter of survival, highlighting a more immediate and palpable consequence of negligence or disregard for established protocols.

As mentioned above, the training to become a qualified skydiver involves a number of levels of difficulty, and each level has to be completed exactly as intended. There is a 100% pass rate; anything below that will prevent you from being permitted to proceed to the next level; there are no short cuts and no middle ground. In saying that, and as in a lot of organisations, people will always try to find ways to take short cuts, therefore as a leader you need to watch out for them. Creating shortcuts may be valuable in some tech industries, where these innovations are cost savers or enhance a product or service, but not in any business where safety is a concern or where a company's reputation or bottom line may suffer.

During our skydiving training one of our team took short cuts, and it almost cost him his life. It also had a massive impact on the rest of us, not just on myself and Kieran, who were in the plane with this friend when the incident occurred, but to the others on the ground watching it all unfold in the skies above. Shortly, and as mentioned at the end of the introduction, I will introduce you to 'Dead Man Walking', but for the moment let's continue with the levels of difficulty our training had placed in front of us.

Training to become a skydiver involves a series of steps and levels of difficulty, each designed to progressively build your skills, knowledge, and confidence. The journey can vary slightly depending on the country and the skydiving centre, but this is how we were taught in the Irish Parachute Club.

Ground Training

- **Introduction to Skydiving:**
  This initial step includes learning about the equipment, aircraft, safety procedures, emergency procedures, and the basics of freefall and canopy control. Ground training typically lasts a full day, starting at 9am and finishing by 5pm, and is essential before making your first jump.

Introduction to Skydiving:

- **First Jump Experience:**
  Back then usually the first jump was a tandem skydive, where you're attached to an experienced instructor. This introduces you to the skydiving experience with minimal responsibility on your part, focusing on enjoying the jump and learning through observation. We had all completed this stage, so there was no need to repeat it.

  Nowadays the first jump is an AFF, or Assisted Free Fall, jump, or direct to Static Line. Occasionally, when the instructors see that the student is a bit unsure of themselves, they will ask them to do a tandem first to get used to the skies, feel a bit of a freefall, check their altimeter (they would have to wear one), try to locate the tandem handle to pull themselves, steer the canopy and locate the landing area.

Solo Skydiving Training Programs

After your tandem jump, if you decide to pursue skydiving further, which we had, you enter a training program designed to take you to your first solo jump. The two most common training programs are Assisted Free Fall (AFF) and Static Line. At this time in 1998 there were no AFF courses in Ireland, so our only option was Static Line. This method begins with a jump where your parachute is automatically deployed shortly after exiting the aircraft, thanks to a static line attached to the aircraft. These are commonly known as 'dope on a rope' jumps, where you're the 'dope', and the static line is the 'rope'.

Nowadays you can choose the following;

- AFF or Static Line and book your training

For both, you would complete a full 1-day ground school class. Depending on your choice these classes are slightly different. During the summer you may actually jump by the end of the day, due to the longer days, but usually you would need to come back some other day for your jump. Your first jump as an AFF is with 2 instructors from 12,000 feet; or as a Static Line is from 3,500 feet.

After several static line jumps that have been completed with 100% accuracy, you progress to 'dummy rip-cord pulls', or DRPs as they were called. These were static line jumps and were designed to ensure that you could find the rip-cord when faced with a true freefall jump. There is no way that you would progress to the next stage, which was freefall jumps with gradual increases in freefall time, leading up to full freefall jumps, if you couldn't find the cord that opened your parachute prior to them releasing the 'dope on a rope'. This is the core proficiency required to jumping out of a plane without the safety of the static line.

Leadership Lesson – Watch Out for the Corner Cutters

But as mentioned before, people find ways to cut corners.

People trying to cut corners, even in life-or-death situations, can be understood through several psychological, social, and environmental factors. Here are some of the key reasons people want to take shortcuts:

- **Risk Perception:**
  How individuals perceive risk plays a significant role. Some might underestimate the danger in a situation, believing that the likelihood of negative outcomes is lower than it actually is. This skewed risk assessment can lead them to take shortcuts or make risky decisions.

- **Overconfidence:**
  Overconfidence in one's abilities, knowledge, or equipment can lead to underestimating the challenges or dangers of a situation. People might believe they can handle the consequences of cutting corners due to their skills or experience.

- **Desire for Efficiency:**
  In many cases the pressure to achieve goals quickly and efficiently can lead people to look for the fastest route to success. This desire can overshadow safety concerns, especially under tight deadlines or in competitive environments.

- **Social and Cultural Pressure:**
  The influence of peers, societal norms, and cultural expectations can encourage risky behaviour. For example, in a work environment where

taking shortcuts is normalized or rewarded, individuals may be more likely to engage in such practices, even when the stakes are high.

- **Stress and Fatigue:**
  In high-pressure situations stress and fatigue can impair judgment and decision-making. When under significant stress or suffering from fatigue individuals might opt for the path of least resistance, which often involves cutting corners.

- **Lack of Awareness or Education:**
  Sometimes individuals may not fully understand the risks involved in their actions due to a lack of knowledge or awareness. Education and training can play a crucial role in mitigating this issue.

- **Cost-Benefit Analysis:**
  People often perform a mental cost-benefit analysis, weighing the advantages of cutting corners against the potential risks. If the perceived benefits (saving time, effort, resources) seem to outweigh the risks, they might decide to take the shortcut.

It's important to recognise that while cutting corners can offer short-term gains or efficiencies, in life-or-death situations, the consequences of such decisions can be catastrophic. Encouraging a culture of safety, proper risk assessment, and ethical behaviour can help mitigate these tendencies.

As mentioned in a previous chapter, short-term gains will not help you if you decide that leadership is a long-term career for you. Building effective leadership takes time, and even at my age I am still learning. Every situation is different because people and culture change all the time, and every leader is a different person, so learning from other's experiences, whilst it might provide you with a guideline on how to manage a particular situation, might not always be suitable to you in all situations.

Skydiving is somewhat different because there is only one way to do it, and it's so important that you take every step one by one. Skipping through training without attention to detail, being overly confident, or just trying to keep up with others (not learning at your own pace so you can absorb all the information and training) can lead to catastrophic consequences.

The first step of skydiving training is to ensure you are mentally prepared for what is ahead of you, and you are fully signed up for the challenge.

The next chapter will delve into the fundamentals of our skydiving training.

CHAPTER 6

LEARNING TO SKYDIVE ON THE GROUND

Learning to skydive is great fun, and the people you meet at the drop zone can often be very exciting characters. They have years of experience, with hundreds and thousands of jumps under their belts, and some fascinating stories to tell. Their key objective however, in this initial interaction with them, is to keep you safe and ensure you have the education, and self-awareness to do exactly that.

There is a full briefing session to start the training off and the instructors make the rules and regulations very clear. The next step is explaining the fundamentals of how a parachute works. The instructors said that there were no stupid questions, so feel free to ask as many as you needed to ask. I started with the first one: 'How long does a parachute last?' This was the answer:

'It's a bit early for you to be thinking about buying a parachute just yet as you really should do a test drive first, but to answer your question, it depends on how you treat it, and how often you use it. If you treat it well, it could last your whole life. If you treat it poorly, it will also last your whole life, however the length of time of said life wouldn't be as long as the one with the well-maintained parachute'

I took my own understanding of this and kept my mouth shut for the rest of the day. I think the reason why was that I was so nervous at the time and didn't want to step out of line, and the way the response was provided set me back a little bit. I know and fully understand that the instructor did not wish to prevent me from asking questions, and his intention would have been to inspire me, and the others, to ask more but it's just how I interpreted it. In fairness, the instructor constantly encouraged us to ask as much as possible, and always said that there was no such thing as a 'stupid' question, but for me I thought I'd filled my quota, so just remained silent.

The fundamental operation of a parachute is centred around the principles of aerodynamics and air resistance, which allow it to slow the descent of a person or object through the atmosphere.

This can be slightly different depending on the type of parachute. The square parachutes, or Ram-Air parachutes, it's aerodynamics first and foremost and air resistance a distant second, however for the old-school round parachutes it's air resistance mostly.

How a parachute works:

Deployment:

The process begins when the parachute is deployed from its container. For skydivers this usually involves pulling a ripcord that releases the parachute from the container strapped to your back. For us during our training and prior to qualifying for freefall, it will be automatically deployed using a cord linking the ripcord to the plane (as previously mentioned, for the 'dopes on a rope'). The initial deployment involves either a smaller pilot chute catching the air and pulling out the main parachute, or the main parachute catching the air, releasing the bungees (elastic bands essentially which are used to tie the parachute into the container) which causes the parachute to unfold.

There are a lot more technical aspects relating to the deployment of the parachute, which include the use of pilot chutes and referring to the ripcord as a handle, or 'hackey', but as this is predominantly a leadership book, I'll try to keep the skydiving tech to a minimum.

Inflation:

As the parachute unfolds it catches air, causing it to inflate and form a large, rounded (often dome-like), or rectangular shape. During my time, I never saw a rounded parachute. These days most parachutes are rectangular because they give the skydiver more control. These are known as 'Ram-Air' parachutes. I think they're called this as the air would effectively be 'rammed' into the cells of the parachute.

Drag:

For the old-school round parachutes the key principle behind its operation is drag, which is a force acting opposite to the direction of motion. The large surface area of the inflated parachute increases the air resistance, significantly slowing down the descent. The shape of the parachute is designed to maximize this effect, balancing the forces of gravity pulling the jumper downwards and the air resistance pushing upwards.

For the Ram-Air, or square parachute the key principle is aerodynamic lift. As cells inflate, the shape of the parachute resembles the shape of an airplane wing. As it flies through the air, the flow of the air above and below the canopy creates aerodynamic lift, which is holding you in the air.

The drag on the Ram-Air parachute does exist but it creates no true value for you. You use the changes in the drag to turn the parachute or to flare.

Flaring can be viewed as increasing the drag to slow you down and make the impact speed slower (for larger student parachutes); or by decreasing the horizontal speed (for smaller sporty parachutes). As your vertical speed is set to zero by changing the angle of attack of your parachute, so your lift is holding you in the air while you are flying parallel to the ground – really hope this makes sense. If not, perhaps you need a 'Skydiving for Dummies' book – this book may seem like one, but it's not.

Stability and Control:

Modern parachutes are designed to be steerable, allowing the jumper to control their direction and speed to some extent. This is usually achieved through vents (on round parachutes) or by manipulating the parachute's control lines, which have steering/breaking toggles at the end. By pulling on these lines, the jumper can change the shape of the parachute and alter its airflow pattern, which can turn the parachute or change the rate of descent.

Landing:

The increased drag not only slows down the descent but with skilled control allows for a relatively gentle landing. Skydivers learn to manipulate the control lines to reduce their speed further just before landing, allowing for a safer touchdown.

For the larger student canopy which I would have used, you pull the toggles to increase drag which slows you down. To a lesser degree the effect described below.

For smaller, and faster canopies which I never had an opportunity to experience, when you pull your toggles, the canopy slows down. Your body (being the most massive part of the body-parachute system) continues to travel forward on inertia, and once it moves forward it tilts the parachute slightly upwards. The parachute is now flying parallel to the ground (and the aerodynamic lift force is holding it). Your vertical speed is zero now, and all your speed is now horizontal.

By applying the toggles more and more you are adding more drag and decreasing the horizontal speed, until hopefully it is becomes zero or very small, and then you touch down, hopefully safely.

Wind direction plays a crucial role in the landing phase of a parachute descent, significantly affecting the approach, control, and safety of the landing.

Skydivers usually aim to land into the wind. Landing into the wind helps reduce ground speed, which is the speed of the skydiver relative to the ground. The slower the ground speed, the softer and safer the landing. By facing into the wind and subtracting the wind speed from the parachute speed helps to decrease the skydiver's speed more effectively as they approach the ground.

The wind's speed and direction influence the skydiver's landing speed and the distance they will travel once they hit the ground. A strong headwind can significantly reduce ground speed, potentially allowing for a more controlled and shorter landing. Conversely, a strong tailwind (wind blowing in the same direction as travel) can increase ground speed, pushing the chute and the skydiver, making the landing faster and potentially more hazardous, requiring a longer distance to come to a stop.

Our instructors taught us that the parachute generally moves forward at 20mph, so therefore if there is no wind, you will need to manipulate the control lines to reduce your speed further just before landing or else you need to prepare for a landing at 20mph, which would probably require a running or 'sliding on your bum' stop. And considering humans are incapable of running 20mph (a 3-minute mile), the bum slide is inevitable. Generally, manipulating the control lines during your landing approach means pulling both lines down fully at the same time, adding more drag to the parachute and reducing your speed – this is called a 'flare'. You should always perform a flare before landing as this is the only way for you to slow your descent; all other factors are outside of your control. One of the more crucial aspects of the 'flare' is timing. The flare must be carried out at an appropriate height above the ground to allow for a smooth landing. The reason for the flare is to increase the drag to slow you down and make the impact speed slower, however if you flare too high and release your toggles after that, your parachute will dive forward (as your body swings back) and you are very likely to hit the ground extremely hard. This could be life threatening. However, if you flare too high but hold the toggles where they were, this is a far safer option. Your body will still swing back and force the parachute to act like a pendulum which means the parachute will go into a dive-recover cycle which will last approximately 10 seconds. If you meet the ground during the dive section of that cycle you will hit the ground hard (but nowhere near as hard as in the first case above).

Imagine it like the letter "J"; whilst in flare, you are positioned along the top section of the letter "J"; when the parachute begins to release some of that extra captured air, you slide down the shaft and swing off the end. If you have no altitude to swing off the end, you hit the ground.

Also in this case, if you cannot flare any further closer to the ground, you will not be able to slow down your descent before touchdown, so should be ready to PLR (Parachutist Landing Roll).

The training teaches you the best way to land if speeds are high or "something happens" on landing (for example a gust of wind). In those instances that I experienced, I always attempted to do as I'd been taught but I usually just ended up on my bum. The PLR training involves keeping your body (and legs) slightly sideways, then on impact roll onto the sides of your calves, then onto the sides of your hips, then bum, back, then opposite shoulder...understand? Yeah, me neither. I always thought I was much more efficient going straight to the bum and skipping all the other steps...or so I told myself.

Sliding on your bum (or feet then bum) does work, but it is not advisable, because there is a risk of breaking your back. I remember a friend of mine saying to me "Perhaps you should just do as we've been taught and stop sliding down the runway on your ass". And he was right. I know he had my best interest at heart, and he said this to me while he was removing a small stone from one of the cheeks of my bum one day; a stone I picked up during one of my 'bum slides'. I accept that the experience of extracting a stone from your friend's backside is probably more harrowing than my part of the experience, so I thought he was only advising me to prevent a recurrence of this, however I didn't listen and decided to stick with it. I fully understood the PLR as the training we were given was excellent, however any time I was in this situation I just naturally went back to what I was comfortable with. Perhaps if I'd just tried it once, and then the next time, I would have become more comfortable, but I didn't. Anyway, I got lucky, never damaged my back thankfully, but had to experience a couple more stone extractions along the way. A small bit of pain in exchange for an excellent uncomfortable experience for a friend...priceless!

When there is a wind it's always important to identify which direction the wind is blowing by watching the airfield's airsock and landing into the wind. The simple mathematics about it is that if you are flying your parachute at 20mph, and being aware that your flare will reduce that speed a little more when landing, flying into a 10mph wind will reduce your speed by obviously another 10mph, allowing for an even slower and safer landing. If you ever notice aircraft taking off and landing, they always face into the wind, and many of us have probably experienced cross wind landings, so you'll understand the impact that can have. Also, birds and other flying animals and insects take the same approach.

So based on this, downwind landings are not ideal and should be avoided, if possible. Jack, who I mentioned was my 'first follower', had a very eventful skydive journey. Over the space of a career of only 9 jumps he experienced more than most of us, including a malfunctioning parachute that needed to be cut away and his reserve deployed, slipping out of the plane when he shouldn't have, and a downwind landing resulting in a very fast stop into some fencing at the edge of a field and cracking his elbow into the side of sheep's face causing some significant bruising to him and probably the sheep as well. Thankfully nothing was broken. We actually don't know how the sheep fared as it disappeared pretty quickly but we all now know how a sheep says 'Ouch'. We were told by our instructors that this was the only place in the world where the sheep looked upwards – this one must have been a rookie like the rest of us.

Although downwind landings may be dangerous they're not considered top of the priority list. Top priority would be to avoid low turns as these can kill you. If given the option to land downwind, or attempt a turn at a lower altitude, you should always accept the downwind landing. The same goes for landing in clear spaces and flaring to at least half brakes. All of these are prioritised higher.

We'll cover Jack's full story a little later, but we were assured in the pub later that evening that this was a first for the parachute club and nobody in its history had ever assaulted any of the farm animals in the area. Or none that there was any proof of anyway. That won't be the only 'first' we brought to this club.

The effectiveness of a parachute depends on several factors including its size, shape, material, and the weight of the load it's carrying. Different types of parachutes are designed for different purposes, such as emergency descents, military operations, cargo drops, and recreational skydiving, each optimised for specific conditions and requirements.

After familiarising us with the fundamentals of how the parachute works, there was so much more to learn. This comprehensive training covered learning about aerodynamics, the other skydiving equipment such as altimeter, reserve parachute and how to deploy, studying emergency procedures and understanding how the automatic activation device (AAD) works, and familiarising ourselves with the processes involved in exiting an aircraft, for which they had a mock aircraft for practice on the ground.

We'll look at each of these now.

1. Aerodynamics:

Aerodynamics in skydiving is a fascinating subject that combines physics and human skill to control movement through the air. When a skydiver jumps from an airplane they enter a realm where aerodynamic forces directly influence their speed, direction, and stability.

Here's an overview of how aerodynamics plays a role in skydiving:

Gravity and Drag

- **Gravity** pulls the skydiver towards Earth, increasing their velocity as they fall. Without any other forces, this would lead to acceleration - continually increasing speed. However, the atmosphere introduces another critical force: drag.

- **Drag** (air resistance) opposes the motion of the skydiver. As the skydiver accelerates, the force of drag increases until it balances the force of gravity, reaching a point called terminal velocity. At terminal velocity the skydiver no longer accelerates and begins falling at a constant speed. The shape and position of the body, the material of the jumpsuit (clothes) and how it fits - loose or tight, can significantly alter the drag experienced and, therefore, the terminal velocity.

- Generally, the rule of thumb is that your first 1,000 feet of freefall takes approximately 10 seconds as you fall towards the ground, and as you reach terminal velocity, each 1,000 feet thereafter takes only 5 seconds. This is important to remember.

Body Position and Control

- The skydiver can control their movement and orientation by adjusting their body position, exploiting aerodynamic principles. Spreading arms and legs or de-arching increases surface area, enhancing drag and reducing falling speed, while streamlining the body or arching does the opposite.
- Movements like arching the back, tilting the head, and adjusting the limbs' angles can create lift and allow the skydiver to move forward, turn, and perform manoeuvres. This is akin to how aircraft control surfaces manipulate airflow to change direction.

Relative Wind

The concept of relative wind (the wind felt by the skydiver moving through the air) is crucial in skydiving aerodynamics. The direction and speed of the relative wind change based on the skydiver's velocity and orientation. Skydivers use the relative wind to their advantage to control their fall and perform various aerial manoeuvres. Remember however that relative wind does not always come from below. On exit from the airplane, the vertical speed is still zero, but your horizontal speed is equal to the aircraft speed, so your relative speed is coming from the side (direction of flying). Again, I hope this makes sense. Think of it like jumping from a speeding car (and please don't try this at home – think about it...don't do it). If you were to jump from a speeding car, you wouldn't land directly below the spot you jumped from – your horizontal speed would keep you moving in the same direction as the car until you hit the road. Again, and seriously, don't do that to test the theory – take my word for it, or look it up somewhere. Isn't there a Google for that type of thing these days?

Stability

Stability in skydiving is about maintaining a desired orientation and controlling movement through the air. A stable position is typically achieved by presenting a symmetrical body posture against the relative wind, allowing for a controlled descent. Uncontrolled movements or asymmetrical body positions can lead to instability, causing spins or flips.

Canopy Aerodynamics

Once the parachute (canopy) is deployed, aerodynamics plays a different role. The canopy acts like a wing, creating lift as air flows over its surface. This lift opposes gravity, significantly slowing the descent.

As mentioned previously by manipulating the parachute's control lines, the skydiver can change the canopy's shape and orientation, altering its aerodynamic properties to control speed, direction, and even perform turns.

Landing

The final phase of the jump, landing, also relies on understanding aerodynamics. The skydiver must reduce their horizontal and vertical speed for a safe landing. This is typically achieved by flaring the parachute (pulling down on the control lines) to increase lift, and also to change the direction of the lift just before reaching the ground, slowing down both vertically and horizontally. Once the control lines are pulled down, the canopy tilts upwards and your body swings forward; the parachute is now flying parallel to the ground (and the aerodynamic lift force is holding it). Your vertical speed is zero now, and all your speed is now horizontal.

By applying the toggles more and more you are adding more drag and decreasing the horizontal speed, until hopefully, it is becomes zero or very small, and then you touch down, hopefully safely.

In summary, aerodynamics is central to every phase of skydiving, from the freefall and performing manoeuvres to controlling the parachute and landing. Understanding and applying aerodynamic principles allows skydivers to control their descent, navigate through the air, and land safely.

2. Altimeters:

In skydiving, an altimeter is an essential tool used to measure the altitude — the distance above the ground level —during the jump. Its primary purposes are to help skydivers know when to perform specific actions during their descent and to ensure their safety from exit to landing.

Here's how altimeters are used in various phases of a skydive:

Exit Altitude

Skydivers use an altimeter to determine the correct altitude for exiting the aircraft. While the exit altitude can vary depending on the type of jump (e.g., progression training, formation skydiving, free flying, or wingsuit flying), it's typically between 4,000 to 15,000 feet above ground level. Knowing the exact altitude helps ensure that skydivers have enough time to perform their planned activities in freefall.

Deployment Altitude

One of the most critical uses of the altimeter is to identify the correct altitude for parachute deployment. This is usually around 3,500 to 4,000 feet for sport skydivers, but it can vary based on jump type and individual preference. In my day, it used to be between 2,500 and 3,500 feet, however they have increased this altitude for safety reasons. Deploying the parachute at the right altitude is crucial for allowing enough time for the canopy to fully inflate and stabilise, giving the skydiver control for a safe descent to the landing area.

Freefall Awareness

During freefall skydivers can lose track of time due to the thrill and focus required for manoeuvres and formations. The altimeter provides constant altitude awareness, helping skydivers make decisions on when to break off from group formations and prepare for parachute deployment.

Emergency Procedures

Altimeters are also vital for executing emergency procedures. If a skydiver encounters a problem with their main parachute they need to know their altitude to decide quickly whether there's enough time to attempt to resolve the issue or if they must cut away the main parachute and deploy their reserve.

Safety and Regulation Compliance

There are specific regulations regarding minimum deployment altitudes and reserve parachute activation altitudes. Altimeters help skydivers comply with these safety regulations and make informed decisions throughout the jump.

Types of Altimeters in Skydiving

- **Visual Altimeters:** Worn on the wrist allowing skydivers to check their altitude visually.
- **Audible Altimeters:** Worn inside the helmet, providing audible alerts at predetermined altitudes. These are particularly useful for freefall awareness and timing, especially when visual checks may be impractical.

- **Electronic Altimeters:** Offer features like logging jump profiles and providing detailed altitude data and serving as your electronic log-book, storing the data of your previous jumps, in addition to basic altitude display.

The altimeter is a skydiver's indispensable tool for altitude awareness and is integral to the planning and safe execution of every phase of the jump. During our time with the Irish Parachute Club we only ever experienced using the visual altimeters, but preferences change as you become more proficient. For us at that time we certainly didn't need anything flashier than the basics.

3. Reserve Parachute

Thankfully I have never needed to use a reserve parachute, however Jack and Sean did. And as Jack said to me just recently, "I think I shit my bags when it happened".(More on Sean a little later).

Deploying a reserve parachute is a critical procedure in skydiving, reserved for situations where the main parachute fails to deploy correctly or when it cannot be used for a safe landing. Knowing when and how to deploy the reserve parachute is crucial for every skydiver as it directly impacts their safety.

Here's an overview of the conditions under which a reserve parachute should be deployed, and the steps involved in its deployment.

When to Deploy a Reserve Parachute

- **Malfunction of the Main Parachute:**
  If the main parachute does not deploy fully, or if it deploys but is not functioning properly (e.g., due to entanglements, tears, or an inability to control it), a skydiver must consider deploying the reserve.

- **Hard-to-Resolve Malfunctions:**
  While some malfunctions may initially seem resolvable, if the skydiver cannot quickly and effectively rectify the situation, it's time to deploy the reserve.

- **Low Altitude with No Parachute Deployment:**
  If a skydiver reaches a critical low altitude without a fully deployed main parachute they must deploy the reserve parachute immediately.

- **How to Deploy a Reserve Parachute**
  The specific method can vary depending on the skydiving equipment and rig type, but the general procedure involves the following steps:

Decision Time:

Recognise that the situation is unrecoverable using the main parachute. This decision should be made quickly, based on altitude and the nature of the malfunction.

Your ground school training will define the decision altitude, by which you need to decide if you can land this "malfunctioned" parachute or cut away.

Time to cure (if curable) is usually: 2 seconds or 2 attempts, whichever ends first...but the decision altitude mentioned above is an absolute priority. For example, if you made 1 attempt within 1 sec and you are at the decision altitude, no more tries. This would purely be in relation to malfunctions.

If you have other problems like a line twist, or side cells not fully inflated, you have more time and attempts, but regardless, at decision altitude such uncured problems turn into a malfunction, and you should cut away. Again, if you do decide to try skydiving, it's probably best to listen to your instructors and pay attention to your training rather than taking skydiving advice from a leadership book – just saying!

Cut Away the Main Parachute (if necessary):

If the main parachute has been deployed but is malfunctioning the first step is often to cut it away. This is done using a cutaway handle found at the front of the skydiving harness. Pulling this handle releases the main parachute from the harness, preventing it from interfering with the deployment of the reserve parachute. I mention 'if necessary' and I mean that it is only necessary to cut away the main parachute if it's been deployed. In some instances, and very rare ones, the reserve parachute is deployed first. Obviously, and I hope this is obvious, there is no way to cut away a reserve parachute because usually this is your last option. But sometimes it's not. More on this later.

Deploy the Reserve Parachute:

After cutting away the main parachute (or if the main has not been deployed at all), the next step is to deploy the reserve. This is typically done by pulling the reserve ripcord or handle, which is also located on the harness. In some modern systems, this action may be linked with the cutaway process, deploying the reserve automatically after the main parachute is released.

At the Irish Parachute Club students are taught to not rely on this process (called RSL - reserve static line) and complete the Emergency Procedure fully, including the reserve handle pull. This procedure is known as 'Look-Locate-Peel-Punch-Pull' and is heavily embedded in students' minds before ever leaving the ground.

Remain Calm and Assume a Stable Body Position:

While deploying the reserve it's important to remain calm and try to maintain a stable body position to ensure the reserve canopy can deploy cleanly and without entanglement.

Prepare for Landing:

Once the reserve is deployed assess its functionality quickly, control your descent if possible, and prepare for landing according to standard procedures.

Automatic Activation Devices (AADs)

Many skydivers use an Automatic Activation Device (AAD) as a safety backup. An AAD is designed to automatically deploy the reserve parachute at a predetermined altitude if it detects that the skydiver is still falling at dangerously fast speed, indicating that a manual deployment has not occurred, or the main parachute has not properly deployed.

Training and preparation are key to effectively handling emergency situations in skydiving. Skydivers practice emergency procedures regularly, including the deployment of the reserve parachute, to ensure they can respond quickly and correctly under stress. Safety is always the top priority, and the reserve parachute system is a critical component of that safety.

4. Exiting the Aircraft

There were a couple of aircraft available at the Irish Parachute Club, and at the time they were Cessnas, either the 182, or the 206. It wasn't too long after I left the club that they invested in a Pilatus Porter which was used as their main aircraft until 2019, and then switched to a PAC750 which is their current main aircraft.

I did most of my jumps from the Cessna 182, which is still in use, and a picture of that exact plane is below,

What you will notice about this plane is the unusual step above the wheel. This is a step, and not a mud guard, and the purpose of this step is to allow the skydiver to 'step' out of the plane, and line themselves up on the 'strut' of the wing. Yes, the preparation done on the ground in the mock up mentioned earlier prepares you to exit the plane at the appropriate altitude, swing your leg out onto the step, reach out onto the strut of the wing, bring out your other leg, and then dangle. Now, that sounds terrifying, right? And it is. It takes a little while, and a few more jumps under your belt to realise that slipping isn't the worst thing to happen to you, because the reason you're up there in the first place was to jump, but it takes your mind a bit of time to come to terms with that.

What you can't see on the strut of the wing is there are two printed hands (I think they were stickers of some sort) to show you where to place your hands, and a little smiley face. The printed hands are in blue so that they are easily seen on the white strut. I remember once that there was somebody learning to skydive at the same time as us (and for the life of me, I can't remember his name). I remember that he was a lovely fella, and in fact sometimes I used to give him a lift back to Dublin in the car at the end of the weekend. He was great to chat with. The one thing I clearly remember is that he was missing three fingers off one of his hands. I never asked him how it happened, but it didn't seem to affect his progression.

It wasn't too long into both of our skydive 'careers' when we had the opportunity to go up in the same plane together. Before I got into the plane with him, and just after I had been selected for that jump, one of the instructors pulled me aside quietly and asked me if I was comfortable with where I had to place my hands on the strut of the wing when exiting the plane, to which I said that I was. He was smiling a little bit, so I wasn't sure what was going on. As we walked out to the plane to board, I was in line to get in first, as I would have been last out on the jump, and I immediately saw that someone had thought it would be funny to put white tape over three of the fingers on the blue printed hands on the strut of the wing. And whoever thought of it was right... it was hilarious. And when this guy saw it too, he couldn't contain his laughter.

The entire journey to altitude was so much fun, and for the first time, I felt my fear of the actual jump begin to subside. It was strange how such an unusual act provided such distraction whilst not actually distracting from the upcoming jump. It gave us all something else to think about, and talk about, while waiting for the door to open.

I'll never forget the fella climbing out of the door, looking back at me with such a great big smile, sticking his only two remaining fingers on that hand towards the instructor in a friendly, 'v' sign, it wasn't exactly a 'v' sign but we knew what he was trying to say, and away he went. It wasn't long until it was my turn, and as I climbed out onto the strut, the instructor said to me, "With all those fingers, you've no idea how easy your life is... now get out there and feck off", and with a smile on his face and a smile on mine too, out I went and off I fecked.

Obviously, in a business scenario, always be careful before taking liberties with your team. Sometimes this kind of fun is not appropriate behaviour. In this environment, that is the way that they behave and it has its purpose. Using humour is an excellent way to keep people engaged and to assist in selling your vision, however the inappropriate use of humour is also possibly the most damaging. (If you haven't watched the TV show, The Office, please do so as this shows you how *not* to use humour in a workplace.)

When I was growing up in the workplace, and working through various different industries, people were always playing silly pranks with others. In a restaurant I was once handed a bucket and tea cloth and asked by the head chef to go to the coffee machine and bring him back a bucket of steam he needed for a souffle. He said just use the steam wand (you know the thing on those machines that's used to heat up your milk). Well, as you can imagine, in front of the whole restaurant, staff and customers, I spent 20 minutes trying to keep the steam in the bucket and because I was so terrified to return to the (usually grumpy) head chef with nothing but a damp bucket I kept trying. Eventually, the manager came up to me and asked me what I was doing and I told him, and he told me that I was holding the bucket incorrectly, so I stood there for another 10 minutes, obviously to no avail.

Other pranks used to be played all of the time, such as asking someone to fetch the long weight from another colleague, and once you asked that colleague for this long weight, they left you standing there for a very long 'wait'. From glass hammers, to lefthanded screwdrivers, to bubbles for the spirit level and jars of elbow grease, the list goes on. And why do we fall for these things? Because we don't know any better and we don't question those around us who we believe havc our best interests at heart.

People did get upset back then, and occasionally there were tears, and although it was all meant in good fun, it certainly did effect people. For me, I learnt to be resilient and my skin became a little tougher. I had a lot of experiences in my past that added to the toughness of that skin, and while I believe it has helped me to this day dealing with people in difficult situations, I also believe it may have blinkered me at times when it came to empathy – I needed to learn to be more empathetic, and not lean on the phrase my father used to say to me: 'Just walk it off son, you'll be fine'

Only a couple of years ago I visited a few friends of mine in Austria who were skiing. They go every year, and although I don't like to ski (possibly because I'm crap at it) I thought it might be a nice few days away and I could join them for the après ski each night. One day they messaged me to say that they had finished skiing and they were in a bar at the top of the ski lift. I left the hotel, one of them skied down the mountain to meet me at the ski lift with a spare pass, as I needed one to go up the lift, and up we both went.

When we arrived at the bar there was a round of beers on the table, all in different coloured bottles and a brand I wasn't familiar with. After we finished that round, I said I'd go the bar to order another round. Two of the guys said they'd have the chocolate one again, another asked for the spearmint, another the strawberry and because mine just tasted like regular beer, I thought I'd stick with what I knew. I went to the bar and asked the girl who came to serve me for two chocolate, one spearmint. I couldn't remember what one of the guys asked for, so I turned back to the group and said, 'Did you want strawberry?' 'Yes', he replied and I turned back to the girl and asked for a strawberry for him and I'll just have a regular. Immediately after I stopped speaking, she looked at me like I had 10 ears, and I turned back to my friends who were wetting themselves laughing. I was so embarrassed, but I got over it quickly when the girl took pity on me, served me the 5 beers, 'ordinary, but with different coloured bottles', and only charged me for 4. She smiled and said, the fruity beers aren't free, but the regular beers are, and she gave me a smile and a wink.

In Feb 2024, as I write this book, I received a message in WhatsApp from one of the guys in the skiing group, and it said, 'chocolate, strawberry, spearmint, and mint Dara', and had the picture below – you be the judge of my stupidity.

Yup, you'd have done it too, right?

These pranks are only found in certain environments these days, and unless you know your audience, be careful. Light-hearted humour is so important but it can go too far. You may think you're the funniest person in the room, but if you're the inappropriate leader and you make people feel uncomfortable with what you believe to be 'funny' comments, it's likely your team won't provide you with honest feedback, like your friends would.

Leadership Lesson – Using Humour as a Leader

Using humour as a leader can be a double-edged sword, offering several advantages but also posing some risks. Here's a breakdown of the pros and cons:

Advantages

- **Enhances Connectivity:**
  Humour can break down barriers between leaders and their teams, fostering a sense of camaraderie and connection. It makes leaders appear more approachable and human, which can encourage open communication.

- **Boosts Morale:**
  Humour is a powerful tool for uplifting spirits and enhancing team morale, especially during stressful times. A well-timed joke can diffuse tension, lighten the mood, and create a more enjoyable work environment.

- **Improves Health and Well-being:**
  Laughter and humour are known to have health benefits, including stress reduction and an improved immune system. Leaders who use humour can contribute to a healthier workplace.

- **Enhances Creativity and Problem-solving:**
  Humour can stimulate creative thinking by encouraging a relaxed and open-minded perspective. Teams that laugh together may find it easier to think outside the box and solve problems more effectively.

- **Facilitates Change and Resilience:**
  Humour can help people cope with change and adversity by providing a more optimistic perspective on challenges. It can be a tool for resilience, helping teams navigate through uncertainties with a positive attitude.

Disadvantages

- **Risk of Misinterpretation:**
  Humour is subjective, and what is funny to one person may be offensive to another. Misunderstandings can occur, especially in diverse workplaces where cultural differences influence what is considered humorous.

- **Undermining Authority and Credibility:**
  If overused or inappropriately timed, humour can undermine a leader's authority and credibility. It's important for leaders to strike a balance and ensure their humour is not perceived as trivialising serious issues or concerns.

- **Exclusion and Alienation:**
  Certain types of humour, such as inside jokes or humour targeting specific groups, can alienate and exclude members of the team. This can lead to feelings of resentment and division within the team.

- **Distraction from Serious Issues:**
  Relying too heavily on humour can sometimes distract from important issues that need to be addressed seriously. Leaders must ensure that their use of humour does not evade accountability or the need for direct action.

- **Overdependence:**
  An overreliance on humour can become a crutch for leaders, potentially preventing them from developing other crucial leadership skills such as empathy, emotional intelligence, and effective communication.

In summary, while humour can be a powerful tool for leaders, it requires careful consideration and balance. Understanding the team's dynamics, cultural backgrounds, and the context in which humour is used are crucial factors in harnessing its benefits while minimising its risks.

After we were familiar with all of the equipment we needed, there was one last piece that we were told about, and something we hadn't thought about. We now knew how to strap ourselves in, enter and exit the plane, we knew how the altimeter and parachute worked, and the importance of flaring when coming in to land, but we didn't know when and how. This was where a radio came in. On the first number of solo jumps, the instructors would ensure you had an earpiece in your ear so they could talk you down after the parachute opened. It's not as simple as just sitting up there and allowing the wind to take you where it desires. You need to be able to get back to the drop zone, and land safely. This wasn't a two-way radio; it was one directional: they spoke, and you listened and you did exactly what they told you. After a few jumps they would slowly take you off the radio, after monitoring your progress and testing your aptitude by allowing you to guide yourself without instruction. Once you proved you were competent, you could jump radio free. My first time jumping without a radio, which I think was my 4th jump, was an interesting story, one which I will go into shortly, but for now, we were all kitted out and ready to go, and it was time to take to the skies.

CHAPTER 7

THE FIRST SOLO JUMP

I thought the two tandem jumps I had done at this stage were nerve wracking, but this was a whole new level. We were only going up to 3,000 feet, and previously I had jumped from 10,000 feet, but this was very different. Firstly, I was on my own and everything about this jump was my responsibility. There was an instructor in the plane, but when I jumped out of this plane, he was going to remain there. Previously with the tandem jumps the instructor was on your back for the entire journey, so if something went wrong, they would know what to do. If something goes wrong now I'll need to fix it. And to be honest, I didn't know whether I would be able to. I kept thinking about the parachute, and whether it would open. I wondered whether I would have the courage to cut away a parachute and open the reserve, if needed.

I had seen this happen once before at this stage (I've seen it a few times since). It happened to my friend Jack during his first jump ever, his tandem jump, and I couldn't get it out of my head. And it was stupid because the likelihood of your first parachute not working was really low, but it happens. The likelihood of both your parachutes not working is extremely rare, and no example of that springs to mind. Yeah, it's true, if the reserve doesn't open, you're in big trouble, but I never understood why I was so worried about it at this time. Perhaps it was just something else to be afraid of. This was terrifying and I'm not afraid to admit it.

I had, and still have, a fear of heights. I had initially decided to do this to try to alleviate this fear, but it didn't work. I remained afraid of heights, but I just found ways each time to overcome this fear. I thought that obviously it's not going to be a quick fix, so I just kept doing it thinking that at some point, I would no longer afraid. A little like your first time trying a pint of Guinness. I don't think I've ever met anyone who liked their first pint of Guinness – some people start with a cordial, like blackcurrant, to add to the drink and make it easier to drink – some just go straight into it and take the hit. Me, I started with blackcurrant and after about 3 pints, I went for it straight and I liked it. The blackcurrant became too sweet, and I wasn't planning to stop after 3, so these were the sacrifices I needed to make. I often wondered why we did this. If something isn't nice at first, why continue to try it? And why try to make yourself like it.

A long time ago, a person I worked with had been a non-drinker his whole life and was now experimenting with the different drinks out there to find his suitable tipple. Another person I worked with suggested Guinness to him. He said he'd tried it and thought it was disgusting and didn't go back to it. The other guy was insistent that he'd like it, as if he intimately knew the complexity of the non-drinker's likes and dislikes, and told him he needed to try a few before he made his decision. 'It's like that new U2 song released last week, the more you listen to it, the more it grows on you'. He looked back in astonishment trying to comprehend what was just said to him. He was a lovely chap, and had a slight lisp, so his response sounded somewhat like this: 'So what you're saying is the reason I don't have a tendency to drink pints of cat's 'pish' is because I haven't drunk enough of it to acquire the taste yet and that I should keep drinking it until I do. If it tastes like cat's pish, then it's cat's pish and that's the end of that'. I understand in later years, long after I no longer worked with him, his favourite tipple became Guinness... he must have passed the 'cat's pish' taste test.

Jack's first tandem jump took place before we all began our 'solo' journey, and as he ascended into the sky, we all watched from the ground. Jack was extremely nervous (or as he would say later, he was always 'shitting his bags'), and to be honest, most of us thought he wouldn't go through with it. Strapped to his back was an Army Ranger whose name escapes me right now, but I remember they used to call him 'Mr. Charming', and I have absolutely no idea why. I never asked and although we all got to know him quite well during our time there, the origin of the name was never found out. He was an extremely competent and experienced skydiver, jumping not only with the Irish Parachute Club but also in his job as a Ranger I recall him telling us of the times he would be part of the team of skydivers who would jump into football stadiums in Ireland and elsewhere – these were the people we'd see on the television, and in hindsight, probably part of the reason why we wanted to do it ourselves. In essence, and blissfully unaware of it at this time, he was probably one of the reasons we were all here.

As we looked to the skies the sound of the plane's engine fell quiet. As mentioned previously, the plane would always throttle down and glide while skydivers were about to exit. This was a good sign, as it seemed like Jack was going to go through with it. It was the point of no return. Then a dot slipped away from the plane 10,000 feet about us – that dot was Jack and Mr. Charming. After 30 seconds of freefall and at approximately 5,000 feet the parachute deployed, and we all started to see it open. But there was a problem. From the ground, the club members murmured, 'it's a line over'... 'he needs to cut'... 'do it Charming'.

One of the experienced members standing beside us quickly explained that it appeared one of the lines had become entangled in the canopy and Mr. Charming was trying to free it, but if he couldn't he would need to use the emergency procedure: cut away and deploy the reserve. The one thing he said that I'll always remember was, 'Don't worry lads, Mr. Charming has him – he'll be fine'.

All of this happened in a matter of seconds. In the sky, Jack knew something was wrong. The canopy was open, but Mr. Charming was behaving in a manner that wasn't explained in the training and his concentration was clearly away from his passenger while he appeared to attend to something else. Jack was obviously worried, and asked, 'We all right?' Mr. Charming responded, 'Just give me a minute'.

Everyone on the ground was right, it was a line over. One of the control lines had wrapped around one end of the canopy collapsing some of the cells used to inflate with air and preventing the canopy from opening fully. There were a couple of problems with this, firstly they were descending too fast and secondly, it couldn't be controlled. There was no other option. As we looked from the ground, the semi-opened parachute just appeared to 'flap' upwards, and we struggled to find the dot as it appeared again significantly lower than the discarded canopy, still falling fast. Although it seemed a lot longer, this was only a matter of seconds. The reserve parachute opened successfully, and the rest of the journey was uneventful... thankfully.

Jack would later say he didn't even have time for 'squeaky bum', but he had plenty of time for it afterwards. From his perspective, initially the main parachute had slowed their descent from 120mph to approximately 35 mph, which is a significant difference. Obviously, as it was his first jump, he didn't know this was too fast and it felt like they were gliding as they should be. He knew from Mr. Charming's behaviour that something was wrong, so he asked again, 'We all right?' But Mr. Charming didn't need a minute as he'd requested. Within seconds of this quick Q&A, Jack felt like a trapdoor had been opened up beneath him, his legs were thrown above his head as he dropped approximately 300 feet in a matter of seconds and the reserve opened. He told me that it all felt like a year. As he continued to replay this event in his mind, he would think about all of the things that could have happened and could have gone wrong, but didn't.

Sometimes we spend so much time worrying about things that will never happen and we second guess decisions we are planning to make. In Jack's case he was second guessing the past and terrifying himself for the future. 'I don't think I can do that again', he said that night in the pub as we dissected every moment of what had happened earlier. As time passed by and more pints were drunk, and members of the parachute club came up to Jack to say, 'Well done' or 'Welcome to the team', or other silly remarks, Mr. Charming came up to him with a glass of whiskey and just said, 'The next time it happens, you'll know what to do. When are you doing your first solo?' Jack looked at him and replied, 'Next week mate', and that was that. At this stage we had all completed our tandem jumps and it was onto our solo training.

I don't know what may have happened if Jack had given up at this stage as he was so instrumental in influencing the others in our group. But he was unfazed and didn't give up. So we continued on our journey - a journey of continued, as Jack would say, 'shitting our bags'.

This was a straight forward static line solo parachute jump. There were 4 of us in the Cessna 182 doing this jump, one instructor watching us, and the pilot. I remember thinking of the old question of why you would jump out of a perfectly good aircraft. And then thinking there's nothing perfectly good about this aircraft. I had been in this aircraft before, but I was already beginning to see things that I had never noticed before. The basics were obvious, like the fact that there was only one seat in this plane and that was used by the pilot – the rest of us sat on the floor. The less obvious things I was now noticing was that the pilot actually wore a parachute too – that's a bit strange, I thought. There was moss on the windows and dirt all around - it didn't look like the air stewards took much pride in their after-flight cleaning. It was a bumpy lift-off and ascent and if there was any wind it could be easily felt in such a small aircraft, unlike any normal commercial airliner. Believe me, if the pilot farted, we'd drift a few feet to the right, but that was the norm, and the experience of being in that aircraft gave you more confidence to jump out of the thing when it was your turn.

When we reached 3,000 feet the door opened and we were ready to go. The pilot stalled the engine and went into a glide. It really gets quiet when that happens. We jumped in the opposite order to the order we got in – first in sat at the back of the plane and was last out. There was no change in order as we all had static lines attached to our parachutes, which were attached to the plane. Any attempt to change order would never be considered because you wouldn't want people to squeeze past other people inside an airplane as small as the 182. The fear would be that you could scrape the back of your parachute against the wall or another person and release the pin - of the main or reserve parachute. If the door is open at that time, your static line can catch air and may pull your Deployment Bag out (or your reserve Pilot Chute may jump out) and can open your parachute - with indeed catastrophic consequences. So, once you were in, that was the order in which you left – last one in, first one out (hate to say it, but some companies still do this with their employees). In fact, on one occasion I was in the plane after I'd completed a few jumps at this stage, and I was still on the static line, and somebody in front of me decided that he wasn't going to jump. Instead of us all moving around, the pilot had to land the plane to let that person out, and then take off again with the rest of us in it. This was one of the many safety protocols that the club were very strict about. I never asked why, but I assume somewhere in their history they had experienced one or more of the catastrophic consequences mentioned earlier, so this rule was put in place shortly thereafter.

Let me tell you this: if you think going up and jumping out is an experience, I advise never experiencing coming back down in the plane. The pilot's response to the jump refusal was, 'Ah, for feck's sake,' and immediately placed the plane into a nosedive pulling up at the last moment to land safely. I remember thinking, this guy must be on a jump-by-jump fee, and not an hourly rate, and I swore no matter how I felt after that, I would never refuse a jump myself. I honestly thought it was safer to jump than to land like that again.

I think I was 2nd to jump so I watched one of my friends go first and carefully climb out onto the step, reach out onto the strut of the wing, dangle his legs and then he was gone. We are told during training how to properly count in preparation for freefall, and the progressions of freefall. The static line assimilated a 3 second freefall, which would be everyone's first freefall if we all passed our progression correctly. Instead of counting 1,2,3, we were told to count 1 one thousand, 2 one thousand, 3 one thousand, which allowed us to properly space our counting to ensure we didn't count too quickly. When my friend jumped first, as he released his hands from the strut of the wing, the instructor kept his head out of the door watching him while myself and the others thought to ourselves, 1 one thousand, 2 one thousand, 3 one thousand. The instructor pulled his head back into the plane and closed the door. The pilot restarted the engine and the instructor looked at us, putting his thumbs up, and said, 'Great jump', and off we went again. The pilot had to regain some of the height lost whilst gliding and a full circle had to be completed so that I would jump out at the same 'spot' as my friend had just jumped from.

A crucial part to skydiving is knowing where to exit the plane to allow you the best opportunity to get back to the drop zone. Experienced skydivers understand windspeeds and altitude and know where the best place to jump from is. Even the most experienced skydiver cannot make it back to a drop zone if they've jumped out at the wrong place in the sky.

And then it came to my turn. It's really such fun sitting in the plane whilst it is regaining altitude and performing a sharp turn in the sky while you're looking out the window, sometimes directly down at the ground. As we reached the 3,000 feet again, I shuffled towards the door and got ready. I gave my instructor the thumbs up, he opened the door to check the spot, told the pilot to cut engines, and this was it. Years earlier and again only a couple of weeks ago I had done this from 10,000 feet with an instructor strapped to my back, but now it was my turn to do it on my own.

Sitting at the edge of the open aircraft door the rush of air and the silence of the engine are all-encompassing. It's a moment of ultimate decision. We were still travelling at about 80mph, and if you can imagine putting your hand out of a car window at that speed, you understand the wind in your face. Then, with a heart full of adrenaline, I put my first foot out and it landed on the step. The next move was to keep one hand on the open door of the plane and reach the other one out to the strut of the wing, and once that's in place, the other hand follows. I placed my other foot on the step, and my instructor shouts, 'Dangle'. I held onto the strut of the wing with all my strength for dear life. In the world of crypto currency, there is an acronym, HODL, which stands for Hold On for Dear Life – this is very different.

I know that it's time to let go, but for some reason I just want to hold on. I know it's only a matter of time until I have to let go, and there's no way back at this stage as the wind is slowly pushing me off the strut, but it just feels safer to hold on. I look to my instructor who is staring at me from the safety of the plane, and with a hand movement similar to what you would see from a marshaller on an aircraft carrier beckoning a pilot to take off, his arm drops 90 degrees in my direction and he says, ‘Go’. I open my hands, releasing my grip. 1 one thousand, 2 one thousand, 3 one thousand.

The static line does its job seamlessly, initiating the deployment of the parachute as I fall from the pane. The transition from the intense noise and chaos of the jump to the sudden, serene quiet of canopy flight is stark and profound. There I was floating 2,800 feet above the ground trying to get my bearings. There are some checks I need to complete, and firstly I look up to ensure that the canopy has opened fully and without problem. It has. Secondly I need to check that the slider is down, which is a small rectangle, usually made of nylon, through which all the lines pass, and which remains above the head once the canopy is fully open. It is. I now need to release the control lines, or toggles, which are fastened to the straps of the parachute with Velcro. Once I release them I can steer. Then I need to figure out where I am.

I understand these days that more and more rigs have moved away from the use of Velcro as it’s not very friendly with the lines. Nowadays the toggles are secured in two small pockets on the rear riser (tabs on each side of the toggle sit in each pocket).

The world looks different from 2,800 feet up, under a fully deployed parachute. It's a period of peaceful descent, offering time to soak in the panoramic views — the tapestry of the landscape below, the curvature of the horizon, and the vastness of the sky around. Steering the parachute, even as a beginner, provides a sense of control and accomplishment. The tranquillity of floating in the air contrasts sharply with the initial leap, offering a unique blend of peace and excitement. All that can be heard is the sound of the wind in the canopy, and nothing else. I can see movement on the ground, and cars passing by, but I can't hear them. It is the most unbelievable experience imaginable. Previously, when I had done my two tandem jumps, the instructor would talk to me, but this was so different.

I hear a voice on the radio: 'All looks good Dara, once you've released the toggles, pull the left one down so I know you can hear me'. I pull down the left toggle and the canopy steers me to the left. The voice says, 'Well done, not let's try it to the right – same again please with the other toggle'. Again, I follow the instruction and the voice recognises my compliance. I was slightly disappointed that another instructor on the ground had ruined my serene moment, but I reckon it's probably best to wait for another time while I learn how to land this contraption and remain alive.

'Now that you're at a high enough altitude, and you're not too far from the drop zone, let's try out a few flares in preparation for landing'. The flare, as mentioned previously, is when both toggles are pulled down together deflecting sections of the tail of the canopy down, thus increasing the drag and reducing speed. When I thought previously that I was experiencing the most serene moments of my life, once instructed to flare, this brought it to a whole new level. Once I performed the flare, the only sound that accompanied me up there, other than the voice in my ear (not the voice in my head telling me I was going to die) disappeared. I have never experienced silence like that. The voice (in my ear) said, 'Well done, try it again', which I did, and then he said, 'Try it a few more times to get used to it', which were the most welcome words, and I had such fun performing this simplest of tasks.

After I'd completed a few, the voice directed me towards the drop zone and ensured that the direction I was coming in to land was into the wind. It was a series of lefts and rights, and I was all lined up and ready. The ground approached faster than you might expect, signalling the need to prepare for landing. The impact of my landing was uneventful, and I needed to add a step or two to balance myself, but did so and that marked the exhilarating conclusion of my first solo parachute jump.

After collecting my gear and receiving a congratulatory handshake from my instructor, there was a moment to reflect on what I've just achieved. The initial fear, the leap of faith, the serene beauty of the descent, and the triumphant landing – each phase of the jump had contributed to a profound sense of accomplishment and a heightened appreciation for the moment.

A first static line parachute jump is more than just an adrenaline rush; it's a journey through a spectrum of emotions and experiences. It teaches lessons in trust, courage, and the ability to embrace the moment, all set against the backdrop of breathtaking views and the unique silence of the sky. It's an experience that leaves an indelible mark on one's memory, often sparking a newfound passion for the sky.

And that was it – I was hooked. We had become full members of the parachute club; and we were welcomed with open arms. The next step was to become full members of the freefall 'club', but there was still a lot of work and training to complete before then. Let's just take one step at a time.

CHAPTER 8

IS IT YOUR CLIQUE OR MINE?

There were a few of us together on this journey, and each of us had our own stories. In this chapter, we'll look at how joining a club or another group, or even a business with a group of friends can have unusual and perhaps unexpected impacts.

Because we'd joined the club as a group it slightly alienated us and prevented us from making friends easily and quickly. Despite us joining an even larger group of people within the club, we would often sit together, eat together, drink together and so on and so forth. This made it difficult not only for us to meet others in the club, but also for others to approach us.

Leadership Lesson – Cliques and what to watch out for

Joining a club or a business with a group of friends and staying within that group has both similarities and differences when it comes to the challenges of making new friends or connections. Here's a comparison of the two scenarios:

Similarities:

- **Comfort Zone Constraints:**
  In both scenarios, being with a group of friends can limit the motivation to step outside one's comfort zone and meet new people, as the social and emotional needs seem to be met within the existing group.

- **Group Dynamics and Perception:**
  Whether in a club or a business, the pre-existing group might be perceived as exclusive or cliquish by others. This perception can discourage outsiders from approaching and hinder the group's members' chances of forming new relationships.

- **Limited Availability for New Relationships:**
  Engaging predominantly with your group of friends means you have less time and emotional energy to invest in new relationships, making it harder to form meaningful connections outside the group.

Differences:

- **Professional vs. Social Objectives:**
  Club: The primary goal is often socialisation, sharing interests or hobbies. The difficulties in making new friends may more directly impact the primary reason for joining the club, which is to engage with others who share similar activities.

Business: Outside of earning a living, the primary objective is professional development and career advancement. While forming connections is still important, it serves more as a means to an end (such as networking for career opportunities), rather than the end itself. The focus on professional rather than personal engagement might make it somewhat easier to bridge gaps since interactions can start on a professional basis and potentially develop into friendships.

- **Structured Interaction:**
  Club: Activities and interactions may be more flexible and informal, depending on the club's nature. This can either make it easier to stick to your group or, in some cases, easier to mingle since activities might encourage broader interaction.

  Business: There's often more structure, with team projects, meetings, and professional networking events that can facilitate forced mixing. This structure can help break down barriers between different groups, making it easier to form connections outside of your initial group.

- **Stakes of Socialisation:**
  Club: The stakes of not expanding your social circle are generally lower, primarily affecting personal satisfaction and enjoyment of the club.

  Business: Not branching out can have professional repercussions, including missed opportunities for career advancement, learning, and collaboration. The higher stakes might motivate individuals to push beyond their comfort zones more so than in a club.

- **Opportunities for Repeated Interaction:**
  Both environments provide opportunities for repeated interactions, which is crucial for forming friendships. However, in a business setting, these interactions may be more frequent and scheduled (e.g., regular meetings or shared/group projects), which can help in

gradually building relationships even if initial efforts are more focused on professional collaboration.

In conclusion, while both scenarios present challenges to forming new friendships due to the comfort and familiarity found within pre-existing groups, the context (social vs. professional) and the nature of interactions (informal vs. structured) can significantly affect the dynamics of expanding one's social or professional network. In a business setting the professional necessity of collaboration and networking, combined with structured interactions, may provide more opportunities and motivation to connect with new people despite the initial comfort of sticking with a known group.

Some of us tried harder than others, and one of us in particular tried harder that the others, and that 'one of us' wasn't me. I enjoyed the comfort and safety of the group. This was an unusual club to have joined because in stark contrast to joining either a golf society or a Weight Watchers class or in fact starting to work in a new company, this club had a very different breed of people and they were quite intimidating, to say the least. Now, this was my perception of these people from within the safety of the group. My perception of these people was somewhat true, but as I very slowly got to know them I realised how wrong I was. As I'll discuss later on, the way that I eventually got to know these people was as a result of my group slowly giving up on the training and deciding to live their lives without the whole 'jumping out of planes' thing.

I learnt from this that not everyone has the same objectives as me. Whilst I was committed to replicating the tandem skydive as a solo jump, not everyone had the same commitment. Some wanted to try it out and then decide, others wanted to place their fear in the background and soak up the atmosphere and the social aspect, because - be under no illusion - the social aspect was fantastic and the nights out after such exhilaration has yet to be topped in my life. And some wanted the same as me.

Leadership Lesson – Understanding Motivations & Objectives

Sometimes in business the very same can happen and it's so important in leadership to understand the differences. By doing so, you can understand the reasons why people are motivated to get up and go into work each day and use these motivations to ultimately influence others.

The motivation and commitment levels across different roles within a company can vary significantly due to various factors such as financial incentives, career aspirations, and the level of influence each role has on the company's direction. Here's a breakdown of how these aspects typically differ among an owner, a CEO, senior management, junior management, and staff:

Owner

- **Motivation:**
  The owner's motivation is often the success and growth of the business since it directly affects their wealth and legacy. They are inherently motivated by the overall value and sustainability of the company.

- **Commitment:**
  As the ultimate beneficiary of the company's success an owner's commitment is fundamentally tied to the long-term vision of the business. Their personal investment (both emotional and financial) usually translates into a deep, enduring commitment.

CEO

- **Motivation:**
  While the CEO may also have a financial stake in the company, their motivation is closely aligned with strategic achievements, company performance, and leadership legacy. They are often motivated by achieving goals, recognition, and, sometimes, preparing the company for future challenges or opportunities.

- **Commitment:**
  A CEO's commitment is typically high, as they are responsible for the day-to-day operations and strategic direction. However, their tenure might be influenced by the board of directors or owners, which can affect their long-term commitment compared to an owner.

Senior Management

- **Motivation:**
  Senior managers are motivated by factors such as career progression, bonuses, stock options (if available), and the success of their departments or projects. Their motivation is also driven by their influence on company policy and strategy.

- **Commitment:**
  Their commitment is often tied to their career trajectory within the company, the success of their specific domain or department, and their relationship with upper management and stakeholders.

Junior Management

- **Motivation:**
  Motivation at this level is frequently related to personal and professional growth, including promotions, learning opportunities, and the success of their teams. They might also be motivated by recognition and the development of leadership skills.

- **Commitment:**
  Junior managers typically have a strong commitment to their teams and immediate responsibilities. Their commitment might be more flexible as they seek opportunities for advancement, potentially within or outside the company.

Staff

- **Motivation:**
  Staff members are generally motivated by job security, salary, benefits, workplace culture, recognition of achievements, and the immediate impact of their work. Personal satisfaction and the ability to balance work with personal life are significant factors as well. Remember that a 20 year old person's motivation is different to that same person at 25 years old, and at 30 years old, and so one. You need to talk with your team regularly to understand how motivations change for each person.

- **Commitment:**
  The staff's commitment can vary widely depending on their career goals, proper position for their skills, satisfaction with their job, and the alternatives available to them in the job market. They might also weigh their commitment against the direct impact they perceive their efforts have on the company.

- **Cross-Role Variations:**
  While these descriptions provide a general overview, it's important to note that individual motivation and commitment can vary widely even within these categories. Personal values, the company's culture, specific industry dynamics, and even the broader economic context can significantly influence these factors. Additionally, the lines between these roles can blur in smaller or more dynamic companies, affecting motivation and commitment in unique ways.

I have tried to correlate each of these roles into the roles each of my group would have represented, but without much success – I suppose a mixture of all of them fits into each person, but I'm not going to try any harder than that. It's important that each of you identify the motivations that every person in your life has and try to identify how this person can influence you and your goals, and also how you can influence them and their goals. Don't discount or dismiss anyone, especially those in your close circle and perimeter or secondary acquaintances. Everyone is in your life for a reason; learn what you can from them and give back where you can. We are both teachers and students at every phase of our existence. Listen without second-guessing. This is not a debate; it's life.

Strangely enough, whilst we unconsciously believed we were safe within our own little clique, the opposite was true. We were all a little apprehensive of the kind of person who would purposely choose to jump out of a 'perfectly good' plane, but we were certain that kind of person was not us. We, on one hand, were crazy enough to try it, some of us crazy enough to want to continue doing it, but none of us knew what the future looked like – maybe none of us would like it enough to continue – perhaps the fear would never leave us – perhaps this would be a very short stay, so we thought it was probably best to stick to ourselves as much as we could.

What we didn't know was that a lot of people recognise a clique pretty quickly and there is a hesitance on their part to get involved. Usually, it's the most forward and over-confident that attempts to gain access. Funnily enough, in the parachute club, there were no real cliques – we had brought our own to the party. In this place where the bar of admittance is just slightly below 'stir crazy', the most over-confident and forward of this group of people is generally the 'bat-shit craziest'. And Conan and Con were the craziest of them all.

Why do people feel uncomfortable joining cliques, and why is it so important to ensure that cliques are not evident in your circle of friends or your organisation?

Feeling uncomfortable about trying to join a clique can stem from a variety of psychological and social factors. Cliques are typically characterized by their exclusivity and a strong sense of internal cohesion, which can make them appear intimidating or unwelcoming to outsiders. We didn't intend for ours to be like this – ours resembled something more of a bunch of cowering idiots all trapped up in a world of self-belief, false bravado and a sense that if we kept to ourselves we could happily discuss our tales of skydiving thinking we were great after doing a couple of jumps without the reality of sitting with somebody who had done hundreds and listening to them tell us how it really was – we were happier in our own little reality.

Leadership Lesson – Cliques, and Why People are Uncomfortable Joining them

However, here are some reasons why people (most normal people and not the 'bat-shit crazy' ones) might feel uncomfortable attempting to penetrate these social groups:

- **Fear of Rejection:**
  One of the primary reasons is the fear of being rejected. The tight-knit nature of cliques suggests that they have stringent criteria for acceptance, making the possibility of rejection more pronounced. The anticipation of possibly being deemed not good enough to join can be a significant deterrent.

- **Social Anxiety:**
  For individuals experiencing social anxiety, the prospect of approaching a clique can be particularly daunting. The stress associated with social evaluations and the potential for awkward interactions can exacerbate feelings of discomfort. As inferred previously, generally 'bat-shit crazy' people do not suffer from social anxiety.

- **Perceived Exclusivity:**
  Cliques often project an aura of exclusivity, which can make them seem unapproachable. This exclusivity can be based on shared interests, backgrounds, or other characteristics that might not be immediately apparent to an outsider, making the idea of trying to join feel like encroaching on private territory.

- **Peer Judgment:**
  The fear of being judged not just by the members of the clique but also by peers outside of it can be a deterrent. Individuals might worry about being seen as desperate or not respecting social boundaries, which can affect their broader social standing.

- **Risk of Losing Individuality:**
  Some people may fear that joining a clique requires conforming to its norms and values, potentially at the expense of their own individuality. The idea of having to change or suppress aspects of oneself to fit in can be unappealing.

- **Status Anxiety:**
  Cliques often have perceived hierarchies or status within a community or social setting. Attempting to join a clique might bring up concerns about one's own social status and the dynamics of power and acceptance within the group.

- **Cultural and Personality Differences:**
  Individuals who perceive themselves as having different cultural backgrounds or personality traits from those in the clique may feel particularly uncomfortable or out of place trying to join. They might anticipate difficulties in relating to or being accepted by the group.

- **Negative Past Experiences:**
  People who have had negative experiences with social rejection or exclusion in the past may be particularly wary of attempting to join a clique. Past traumas can heighten the fear of experiencing similar pain again.

Navigating these social dynamics requires a delicate balance of self-confidence, social skills, and sometimes, a strategic approach to building relationships. Overcoming the discomfort often involves recognising one's own value and finding common ground with members of the clique, all while maintaining authenticity, respecting personal boundaries, and preserving friendships outside the clique.

Our clique was nothing like the above. I honestly don't think that anybody in the parachute club was worried about being rejected by us or being judged or even losing their own individuality – I think they just couldn't care less. Although they didn't have a bunch of individual cliques within the club that they felt they needed to join, they were all in the same one – The Irish Parachute Club; this was their clique and they were all members. We were just a separate entity looking in, and they just couldn't have been bothered trying to join us.

We noticed over the weeks that the people who joined the club at the same time as us, who would join us for our training, were able to tell us more about what was happening in the club because the members welcomed them in with open arms. They sat together, they ate together, they drank together – it was just us who created that divide. And perhaps that was a reason why the craziest of them all approached us one evening in the bar and said, 'Hey guys, I'm Conan and this is Con'.

Conan was originally from Offaly, where the parachute club was located. Offaly is in the midlands of Ireland, and the people from this county have the nickname 'BIFFO' – which stands for '**B**ig **I**gnorant **F**ecker **F**rom **O**ffaly'. Conan perfectly exemplified this nickname. He was a large personality as well, and an extremely charming man. He had some fantastic stories, and although most of them were about skydiving, the rest of them were about his prowess in bed with the 'ladies' – I place a '' around the word ladies, as we all honestly believed that some of these stories may also have been about sheep, but we'll never know. And if I was being totally honest, I don't believe the majority of these stories were true, but as we all know in Ireland, 'Never let the truth get in the way of a good story'. He was a large man and I'm not quite sure what he did for a living – not that I've forgotten; I just don't think we ever asked. In this place, nobody cared about what you did on the outside. Perhaps that's what prison is like. I've yet to experience it and will happily avoid that environment, but in this place, everyone was equal. We all had the same thing in common, so it didn't matter if you were the Chief Executive of a multinational conglomerate or a waiter in a coffee shop, everyone was treated equally. There was no tolerance for, or in fact time to waste on irrelevant details such as those – we all wanted to survive the weekend of jumping and get back to our lives so that we could return the following weekend. External status had no place here and we were truly 'all in it together'.

Con was probably only 5 feet 4 inches tall and as he would say to any who would listen, 'I may be small, but my mickey is huge' – I've often thought about him over the years and wondered what he was doing now – either a porn star, or sharing a bunk with Harvey Weinstein I would think. Con was a fascinating character and so funny. As far as I remember he was from

West Dublin, and although nobody asked about what people did on the outside, I think Con was in the printing business. I know this because he used to talk about how often he would take blurred photocopies of his genitalia (this guy was doing things with pictures long before Photoshop) and 'accidently' include them in printing packages that were given to customers and clients. Apparently, people used to complain about some blurred copies of some of the printing material, but they were never sure what the image was, and neither was Con's boss when the images were returned to the printing shop. It was usually shrugged off as a technical issue. Con would say, 'Ha ha – technical my balls'. Nobody needed to know – once he knew, that was enough.

We were a bunch of middle class, South Dublin, relatively well-educated young people, and when presented with both of these characters, we were instantly in awe of them. We sat mindlessly engrossed in their stories of skydiving, ladies (sheep) and photocopying what should be 'unphotocopiable'.

Not only did these two characters become a part of our little clique when we were at the club, but they also joined us at home too, and would come out with us into our local bar and crash out on someone's sofa at least once a week.

There was nothing off limits with these two; their entire life was about having fun. There are so many ridiculous stories from our time with these two, and probably too many to go through, but here are a few of the highlights. Now granted, I'm not saying that these are things that you should try at home... I'm just saying these are things that we did. These things were normally fuelled by a ridiculous sense of bravado and a feeling that nothing could kill you and were usually done whilst under the influence of a significant amount of alcohol. Whilst the parachute club was extremely stringent on safety, the social aspect that we became involved in was purely drinking alcohol and doing very stupid things. The club has changed a lot since then, and from speaking to members of the club nowadays, although they have heard the stories from back then, and enjoy hearing them, they have very little tolerance for this behaviour now.

Looking back I recognise how stupid we were back then and I'm certain that if I decided to take the stories I read from a book, like perhaps you may be thinking right now whilst reading this book, and replicate them, that would put me on a whole new level of stupidity. So please don't!

The trip to Rathangan

There was a nightclub in a small town called Rathangan in County Kildare, which was only about 10km from Clonbullogue. Occasionally, after a night in the local pub some of us would go there to find more ways to destroy our livers. The nightclub was a funny place where all of the beers were served in cans, not glasses. I'd often thought that we'd have been better off staying where we were and buying a few cans of beer from the pub, but I suppose that would have been more sensible than driving to Rathangan. As I've mentioned, being sensible was not on our radar much those days.

Conan was driving and, thankfully this night, he hadn't been drinking. I can't fully remember everyone who was in the car, but I was in the passenger seat at the front, another guy called Tim was in the back behind the driver, Con was also in the back behind the me, and there was someone in between them in the middle seat. During the 11-minute drive, Con decided that he wanted to sit in Tim's seat and wanted Tim to swap with him. They were both quite drunk. He immediately lowered the window on his side of the car and started to get out while we were driving through the country roads at speed. Before he got out fully, he dropped back inside the car and said to Tim, "Well?" And without asking Tim appeared to know exactly what he wanted to do. I remember thinking, they've obviously done this before.

Tim responded immediately by rolling down his window and climbing out onto the roof on his side, whilst Con did the same on his. Thankfully there was a roof rack on top of the car so they had something to hold onto, but the strangest thing about it all was that nobody else in the car, including me, attempted to stop them – they all thought it was hilarious; I think I was just shocked. This was a whole new level of crazy. At around 12:20am on a Saturday night sometime in 1999, in the middle of nowhere in the Irish countryside, this car was travelling down the middle of a small country road at 80kph, three stupid people on the inside of the car, and two even more stupid people hanging onto the roof rack on the top.

Con was quite small, so he went under, and Tim went over... from the inside of the car we heard something unusual, like a snap, but we weren't sure what it was. Tim tells the story better, "I remember a small hanging branch cracking into the top of my head as Con and I swapped. It felt like I'd been hit by a baseball bat, but I hung on for dear life and it was exactly then that I realised that this was not a very smart idea. I managed to continue to hold on and I could feel the blood from my head dripping down into my eyes whilst I tried to navigate the entry back into the car. Con was already back inside the car in the seat I had been sitting in only a few moments earlier, but I was struggling".

Conan had no idea that Tim had been hit by a branch, and he thought it'd be funny to start to swerve the car back and forth on the road. As he would say later, 'Sure, you were making it look too easy'. As the car swerved from side to side, Tim managed to pull his legs down the side of the car and then as he pulled the steering wheel to the right, Tim's legs swung away from the body of the car into the night air and the only part of him attached to the car were his hands on the roof rack. This swerve only lasted a second as these were not very wide roads, but as he would say later, "it felt like an hour as I thought my hands were going to slip". As he swerved back in the opposite direction, Tim's legs came crashing back to the side of the car. He managed to pull them up into the window and he was back inside the car. I turned in my seat to look at him and his face was covered in blood. Con said "oh, that doesn't look good mate", and Conan said he'd a first aid kit in the car.

We arrived in Rathangan a few minutes later, and before we could go into the nightclub, Conan pulled out the first aid kit he kept in the car, probably the wisest decision he ever made was to buy one of those, and did a quick patch up on Tim's head. We went in, enjoyed the rest of the night and drove back to Clonbullogue later – everyone stayed in the car for the entire journey this time however, and that was the only time I ever saw anything as stupid as that, and I've seen some stupid things down there. I believe Con took up 'car surfing' as a hobby and started getting quite good at it. It was a solo career for him as he never could find another person as stupid as Tim to do it with him.

The following morning at the drop zone, people asked what had happened to Tim's face and head.

'The 'fecking eejit' got hit by a tree last night'. The others in the club looked at Tim and obviously thought, well that's plausible, and they accepted it. How do normal people believe a story about a tree assaulting someone? It wasn't that he'd fallen into a tree, or that he'd accidently run into a branch, or in fact the truth of how it actually happened (we probably would never have admitted to the truth). They all accepted that a tree hit him – what else didn't I know about the Irish countryside, and should I be watching out for aggressive trees now as well?

There was already a lot of other things to watch out for and we were still only learning this skill, so distracting myself with other nonsense and these crazy people probably wasn't a good idea.

One last story about another one of the characters in the club and the way in which he was perceived. He was called the Perv and was a hilarious character with a million funny stories. Everyone in the club liked the Perv. The last thing I remember about him was that he had a horrific accident one day where he broke both of his legs coming in to land. He tried a high-speed turn at a very low altitude, ended up crashing into the ground, and he was rushed to hospital – to be honest, I think that was the last time I saw him. He was wild and reckless and took lots of chances and finally one of them caught up with him. A nice guy who I believe is doing well for himself these days, but he lived life right at the edge.

When we first met him we were introduced to him simply as the Perv, and instead of asking him directly we asked somebody else why he was called that, and that person said that he would tell us himself when he got to know us a bit better, so we waited until that time. Nobody else would tell us, so we had no other option. This certainly intrigued us because generally there were always rumours and suggestions about people, but nobody would talk about this. One guy I remember was a lovely shy quiet guy who openly admitted that he hadn't had a girlfriend for about 2 years – obviously the rumour began to spread that he must be gay. In fact, without any evidence to suggest this rumour was true, people started to call him gay, which he always denied. It didn't matter to be honest, and in my opinion, I don't think he was, but the nickname stuck. So, after some time of getting to know the Perv, he finally told us the story about why they all called him 'the perv', and given the fact that some guy was being outed as gay for no apparent reason, we all thought that this was certainly going to be an interesting story.

To keep it short, the Perv had been in Bangkok a couple of years previously and he came back to the club with this story. As he was walking the streets of Bangkok, he was approached by 2 beautiful Asian girls who started to proposition him. The Perv was instantly interested as this was the very reason he was walking the streets of Bangkok – so handy I remember him telling me. 'I hadn't walked 20 yards at this stage', he said. Obviously, being a man who was inherently allergic to spending money, he started to haggle the price and after they agreed on an appropriate rate, the Perv walked off with them to wherever it was they were taking him. As he walked away with them, a couple of Irish lads had been watching him, and shouted across the street to him, 'Hey pal, they're blokes... you know that?' With all of the Perv's extraordinary confidence, he said, 'Oh yeah pal, I know that – only a man knows how to truly satisfy a man' and off he went. I couldn't believe my ears – I asked him whether he did the deed or not and he quite openly said that he did and he said it was the best experience of his life and would definitely do it again.

I honestly couldn't believe what he was telling us and everyone was laughing, and all I could think about was the poor guy who had been labelled as gay purely because he hadn't had a girlfriend for some time, and the Perv had openly admitted to having a sexual experience with not just one, but two other men, and he was nicknamed 'the Perv'.

After hearing the story and everyone now knowing that the Perv had told us it, I asked some others about it, and all of their responses were the same, 'Oh no, the Perv's not gay... that's for certain... he's just a filthy pervert!'

These people were the strangest group I'd ever had the pleasure of knowing.

CHAPTER 9

LEARNING THE ROPES

Each of us had a different journey as we learned the ropes of this extreme sport.

People pursue skydiving for a variety of reasons, spanning from personal growth to pure thrill. I spoke to many people in the club during the time I was there and here are some of the most common motivations; some of these motivations were also some of mine:

- **Adrenaline Rush:**
  Skydiving provides an unmatched adrenaline rush. The excitement of freefalling at speeds of over 120 mph is a powerful lure for thrill-seekers. I would have to admit that since I had completed the initial tandem jump I did in 1994, this was a huge part of my motivation – I wanted to replicate that feeling on my own.

- **Conquering Fear:**
  Many see skydiving as a way to confront and overcome fears, particularly the fear of heights. It's a step outside of one's comfort zone, proving to oneself that they can face and conquer their anxieties. This too was a motivation of mine, and to be honest, it never worked – I'm still as afraid of heights as I ever was.

- **Sense of Freedom:**
  Skydiving offers a unique sense of freedom that's hard to find elsewhere. The experience of flying through the air can feel liberating and exhilarating. This was never one of my motivations for starting this journey, however it was definitely one of the reasons why I kept doing it. This sensation cannot be matched anywhere else.

- **Achievement and Accomplishment:**
  Completing a skydive is a significant achievement for many. It requires a certain level of bravery and commitment, and successfully completing a jump can provide a great sense of pride and accomplishment. Initially, I wanted the achievement of completing a jump, but this wasn't a reason for continuing with the journey.

- **Perspective and Relaxation:**
  Despite the initial adrenaline rush, many skydivers find the experience incredibly peaceful and meditative. The moment of canopy flight is often described as serene, offering stunning views and a unique perspective on the world. Similarly to the sense of freedom, this aspect was a reason for continuing on the journey, and again this sensation is hard to match anywhere else.

Leadership Lesson – Remaining Calm in a Crisis (part 1)

Often in times of crisis as a leader I say to people, 'Have you pulled your ripcord yet?' What I mean by this is, have you got a calm perspective right now and are you relaxed? If you are still experiencing the adrenaline rush of the cause of this crisis, similar to the adrenaline rush from a skydive at 120mph, this is not a good time for you to make important decisions. Adrenaline or emotionally fuelled decisions, rarely work out well – quite often there is no time in business to calm yourself, and decisions are needed instantly; you need to find a way for yourself to compartmentalise the adrenaline and emotions, and make your decisions based purely on facts or data. This can be very difficult to achieve. What I find helps me is mentally returning to that time while floating in the clouds, without a sound in the world and no distractions. The solution often becomes apparent. At the very least, it calms me enough to be able to think clearly, making it easier to see a path to resolving the issue. I hate the expression 'happy place', but this is mine, and you should find yours.

- **Social and Community Aspects:**
  The skydiving community is known for being welcoming and supportive. Learning to skydive opens up opportunities to meet new people, make friends, and become part of a community with shared interests. This became a massive part of our journey, and although there is no way that I would be able to keep up with the pace of this social life at my age now, I loved every minute of it. I'm surprised I survived it (possibly more dangerous than the jumping itself) and I don't regret any part of it at all.

- **Physical and Mental Challenge:**
  Skydiving is both a physical and mental challenge. It requires a good level of physical fitness and mental preparedness, making it a comprehensive activity for those looking to push their limits. I wasn't too worried about the fitness side of this. Although it does require some physical fitness, it's not exactly the most strenuous activity – how hard is it to fall? Although you need good upper body strength to steer and land and good stamina in general, you most certainly need to be mentally strong. Some of the group I joined the club with probably weren't as prepared as they should have been. In hindsight though, maybe they were exactly as prepared as they needed to be, because this

isn't for everyone. Perhaps it would be fairer to say that they weren't as mentally prepared as I was to do skydiving – most of them were more mentally prepared for everything else in life than I was at that time – but that was their choice. As I mentioned earlier, we all had a different journey and different reasons for doing this.

- **Professional or Competitive Interest:**
  Some are drawn to skydiving for its competitive aspects, including formation skydiving, free flying, canopy piloting, and more. Others may pursue it as a career path, working towards becoming instructors, videographers, or performing jumps for entertainment or demonstration purposes. Nah, none of this was for me, but many people in the jump wanted to pursue this as a career. Some also used it as an addition to their current career, such as Mr. Charming, who was an Army Ranger and who skydived for a living. He used this as a way to continue to improve his skills and also as an added income – he would get paid to bring people up for tandem jumps and other activities he would do for the jump.

- **Life Perspective:**
  Experiencing the intense moments of a skydive can alter one's perspective on life, making everyday problems seem smaller and encouraging a more adventurous and appreciative outlook on life. This was a result of my experiences and not a motivation. As mentioned above, this experience helps me to calm everything down when confronted with a crisis. Over the years I have always been regarded as the calmest person in the room in a crisis – if only they all knew that I was just drifting through the clouds in my head.

- **Bucket List Achievement:**
  For many skydiving is a bucket list item — a once-in-a-lifetime experience they want to try. The idea of doing something so extraordinary is a powerful motivator. I had met a lot of people who wanted to

complete one jump and that was it. If I'm totally honest with myself, perhaps the one I did in 1994 was my bucket list jump, but as I continued, it no longer became valid as a motivational reason to do this.

Each individual's reasons for skydiving varies, sometimes widely. Often, it's a combination of these factors that drives someone to take the leap. Each of us had our own and we really only ever shared these reasons at a much later date – years after we'd all finished this 'lunacy'.

In amongst the craziness that the skydiving lifestyle brings with it - for all you skiers out there let's refer to it as 'après dive' - there was the serious side of progressing through our training and achieving our own personal goals. During this chapter, I'll go through the stories of each of us as we faced our fears together and overcame our own personal challenges. Not everyone of us completed the training and achieved full skydiving qualifications, but each one of us had both individual and collective experiences that will remain in our memories for the rest of our lives. Even to this day, occasionally (and very occasionally I might add), a skydiving story is revisited. As with all groups of friends, there are memories that you share and sometimes mistakes you make that your friends will always be delighted to tell you about.

Taking a left to Magaluf

I digress slightly while I remember an incident on the island of Majorca that took place many years ago. A large group of us, a mix of boys and girls, went on a summer holiday together to this beautiful island, as probably a lot of people did in their younger years. We were staying in a resort called Santa Ponsa, and to every Irish person who has ever been there, it was nick-named 'Ballymun in the Sun' because of the similarity to Ballymun with its high-rise flats. Those of you reading this from Ireland will understand.

Whilst in Santa Ponsa, we took a collective decision to hire some mopeds and drive to Magaluf, which was only a 10- or 15-minute drive across to the other side of the island. Santa Ponsa was predominantly an Irish resort, whilst Magaluf was an English resort, but that's not really relevant to the story.

The trip was simple – up the road, reach the motorway and turn right... that was it. Kieran decided not to hire a moped and went for a car instead – I think he chose a SAAB 900 convertible which was a lovely car back then. Two of the girls then decided to join him in the car and the rest of us hired mopeds. As we embarked on our quick journey to Magaluf, we all followed Kieran in the car as he had studied the map in more detail than the rest of us. As you will hear later about Kieran, he is a very meticulous person who pays great attention to detail, so we took his lead. When we reached the motorway, there was an option to turn right onto a smaller road, which we believed would lead us directly to Magaluf, however Kieran disagreed and insisted that we take a left. With no reason to argue, and with the comfort in knowing that Kieran was usually right about these kinds of things, we all turned left and joined this large motorway, which, to be honest, was a little scary on a small moped. To cut a long story short, due to the nature of the road, and the speed of the traffic passing us by, one of the girls fell off the moped, totally destroying both herself and the moped; the journey was cut short as she needed to be brought to hospital and the rest of us had to arrange to deliver the written off moped back to the hire centre and explain what had happened.

After initially being very concerned about the health of our friend who had taken the fall - she was fine... just a few cuts and bruises - the owners of the hire centre asked us what happened and it became apparent very quickly that we should have taken the right at that junction, not left, and we would have made it to Magaluf quite safely. One of the staff at the centre said something like 'Crazy Irish... never listen... we told you to take a right', and he was right. I knew that I hadn't listened to a word he'd said myself. I had put my trust in someone else doing so, and it appears that none of us did – well there's definitely a learning from that.

Anyway, for the rest of the holiday, poor Kieran was subjected to such ridicule. The slightest little thing he would say or do for the rest of the holiday would create a mini competition for the rest of us to see who would land the quickest joke. "Right, I'm off to bed", "Did you mean to say 'Left, I'm off to bed'?". There were many more of them, but get the idea.

We were a mature bunch back then. However, even to this day, these things are not forgotten. About 6 weeks ago, a few of us, including Kieran, were travelling in the same car together through a part of Ireland. We were looking for a local shop. Kieran said that he knew the town we were driving through, and he said that the shop was just up the road on the left. Of course, the quip from the back was 'Up on the left... up beside Magaluf, you mean?' I guess we still haven't grown up much, but it was hysterical, and we felt like kids again laughing all the way – you'd have to have been there.

Anyway, back to learning the ropes. The process was simple: you needed to complete 5 'dope on a rope' jumps in a row without any mistakes. If you made a mistake, you started from the beginning again.

All that was required for these jumps was to climb out onto the step above the wheel, hold onto the strut of the wing, dangle your legs and let go. You needed to fall from the plane aerodynamically, therefore you would arch backwards, spread your legs, so that you almost created a star formation, and just let go. The 'rope' would do the rest, and you would follow your canopy opening procedures, and checks, as you descended towards the ground.

Whilst under the canopy, the instructors on the ground would direct you on the one-way radio to help you with directions and other methods of canopy control which have been already discussed in this book. A part of this stage was the progression from 'on radio' to 'off radio' when you no longer needed to be guided from the ground and were competent enough to be able to find your own way back to the drop zone.

Once you completed those jumps, you progressed to the 'dummy ripcord pull'. This was the jump where your parachute was still attached to the plane, but rather than just jumping out and letting the parachute open you had to perform the actions of pulling a ripcord, which is what is used to open the parachute, and to show the instructors that you are able to find it and successfully pull it. This was just a piece of plastic attached to a handle and was placed in the same position as a regular ripcord would be. The reason for this is that the next stage was freefall and if you couldn't find the ripcord whilst the parachute was going to open for you itself, you would definitely not progress to freefall. As an instructor once said, "If you can't open your parachute, who do you think is going to do it for you?"

As this was just a piece of plastic and not a part of the rig itself, generally as you pulled it, when the parachute opened itself a part of your canopy process was to place this piece of plastic in your mouth for the ride down while you used both hands to steer the canopy. In fact, there was nowhere else to put it really.

The other difference with this jump was the change in position as you fell from the strut of the wing. Because it was so important to remain aerodynamic, you couldn't just pull one hand down to pull the cord because the other hands still stretched out in the form of a star would catch more wind and spin you into an uncontrollable position. Therefore the process that had to be followed to keep yourself aerodynamic was that once you let go of the strut, you did a 3 second count (one one thousand, two one thousand, three one thousand), and on the third 'one thousand' as you pulled down your right hand to pull the ripcord, you brought your left hand into your forehead so that your protruding elbows kept you aerodynamically sound. So rather than your hands keeping you balanced, because you were using one hand to come in towards your body to pull the cord, you needed to counter balance with the other hand allowing your elbows to do the heavy lifting, otherwise you would flip around and potentially open your parachute while your back was facing the ground, which is not ideal for the successful opening of a parachute.

The parachute is on your back so that nothing gets in the way of it opening – if you allow yourself to get in the way of it opening, there are just too many things that could go wrong. The instructor watches your actions from the door of the plane to ensure that you reach the cord, and then they close the door, usually giving a thumbs up to the other people in the plane, the pilot throttles back up the engine, and they circle back to the spot again for the next person to jump. Once you land the instructors on the ground ensure that the ripcord is still in your mouth, and if both accounts tally up, that is a successful jump and you progress to the next jump in this stage. This stage also requires 5 perfect jumps before you progress to your first freefall.

Now freefall is a whole new kettle of fish, however your first is almost like an initiation into the world of skydiving. It's almost like passing your driving test and throwing away the learning plates once and for all. And the night after your first freefall is a graduation celebration in the pub, involving all members of the club. It's a ceremony that is most definitely not for the faint-hearted, and yes, as you can probably guess, involves a wee bit of alcohol. Only 3 of the four initial group made it this far, and I'll shortly tell you of each of our journeys. However I did, and here's what happened that night.

In preparation for the ceremony, each new 'freefaller' needed to bring a bottle of something with them. This something had to be alcoholic, and couldn't be a soft drink, but the choice was yours.

Irish Cream Poitin

My choice was a bottle of poitin (Irish moonshine), made with Irish Cream, rather than just Whiskey. Somewhat like a Bailey's Irish Cream, but a hell of a lot stronger. Almost like the Conor McGregor of Irish Cream... it sounds dreadful, has a shockingly bad attitude, and will definitely knock you out if you don't treat it with respect. The reason for this choice, I'll explain. I have never, ever seen a drink like this anywhere in the world, and it was absolutely beautiful. This drink was not available over the counter, and was specifically made in the mountains of Monaghan by God only knows who.

In the place I was working at the time (I was a security manager in a large retail outlet), a wonderful man, whose name totally escapes me, would come to the store to collect the very large rubbish skip that was kept out the back of the store. From many conversations with this man, I discovered that he knew someone in the Monaghan mountains who had their own 'unofficial' distillery and made homemade poitin, and this Irish Cream was made from said poitin... and the best part of it was that it only cost a tenner.

Prior to bringing this down to the club as my 'freefall' bottle, I had previously bought a few of them, and between myself and some of my friends, we had many a forgetful night (they were not forgettable, we just couldn't remember them), so I thought it would be perfect for this bunch of high-flying lunatics. As I came closer to my first freefall I bought a bottle from my 'skip' friend and stored it away. Now because this wasn't an actual distillery, the bottles this poitin came in were my very first experience of recycling – you never knew what kind of bottle it would be delivered to you in. It could be an unused bottle of Jameson, Hennessey... anything, and it wasn't actually sealed.

There were two rules for this bottle in the club. One: it had to be a brand-new bottle and had to be sealed. I managed to bypass this rule when I explained to them that it was poitin, and instantly they all seemed to be quite happy to disregard that rule. The second rule was that the bottle needed to be covered, in full, with masking tape. There could be no sight of the bottle, or the label, just the cap and a bottle shape roll of masking tape. Why, you may ask? I thought that it just added to the intrigue of it all, but the reason the bottle was wrapped in masking tape was to allow all of the members of the club to write a message to you – perhaps something similar to a graduation book in schools in the US, or how people sign a cast when someone has broken a limb – not the best analogy for a club like this, but you know what I mean. The bottle gets passed around the members of the club that night in the local pub, and once you take a swig, you have to sign the bottle.

I still have my bottle...

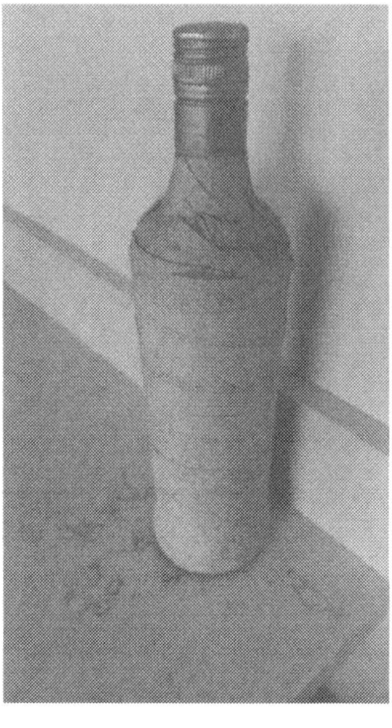

...as you can probably see, the writing is very hard to read these days purely due to the length of time I have this bottle. For years I used to look at it and remember all the great characters at the club. The bottle used for this poitin was an old peach schnapps and initially when I brought the bottle out there was a lot of teasing about the choice of drink I had brought with me because all the others could see was the peach schnapps lid. Believe me, when they took a sip, those teasing faces changed instantly. That put a little smile on my face. Never judge a book by it's cover, as they say.

While this is going on, the members of the club have other plans for you. As part of the initiation, you need to buy, yes, you have to buy it yourself, a half pint of your choice of beer, and a shot of anything alcoholic. My choice was a half pint of Guinness and a shot of Jameson Whiskey (I know, typically Irish – I couldn't have been more Irish with that choice). When served to you, the member of the team would hold you upside down, and you had to drink both drinks without spilling anything. If you spilled anything, you needed to do it again, and again. I got it right the first time, thankfully.

I once saw someone having to do it 6 times, and he still didn't get it right, but they gave him a reprieve after the sixth attempt – everyone had just gotten bored at this stage. I also remember that he wasn't allowed to jump the next day for obvious reasons. I often thought that I probably would have 'accidently' spilled some of it if the club was paying for the drinks, but because it came out of my pocket, I just did it the first time and sat back upright again and enjoyed the rest of the night.

Sean and I did our initiation ceremony on the same night... Kieran had done his a few weeks earlier. All of us passed on the first attempt – I think we were just brought up to know that it's disrespectful to spill any alcohol in Ireland, so we just didn't. In hindsight, maybe we should look at how we were brought up, in fairness.

Our Skydiving Experiences

We each had our own experiences, and although we may not all have made it to freefall that doesn't necessarily mean that we all didn't achieve our goals. I used to look back and sometimes think that the friends in our group who hadn't progressed to freefall like Sean, Kieran and I had somehow failed; had not achieved what they had set out to do. But this view is a very short-sighted view. It's a view that comes from my own mind perspective, and it's unfair to judge others' successes or failures based on my perspective. Everyone has their own goals to achieve, and although those goals may not be the same as mine, and they may be higher or lower, they are still goals and achievements that should be respected. If you go back to thinking about the goal of just achieving one parachute jump, well then everyone of my friends achieved this, and well done to them. It was me who moved the goalposts after the first jump and settled them at the level of freefall – not the others. In fact, as the story continues, although I may have been critical about the achievements of others, I would end up eating my own hat, and deservedly so.

Leadership Lesson – Recognising the Goals of Others

In leadership recognising that different people have different goals is crucial in fostering a respectful and collaborative environment, whether in sports, the workplace, or personal relationships. This understanding is important for several reasons:

- **Encourages Diversity of Thought:**
  Understanding that others might have different aims allows for a broader range of ideas and perspectives. This diversity can lead to more innovative solutions and more interactive team dynamics.

- **Enhances Teamwork:**
  In a team setting, knowing that members might have varying objectives helps in aligning their efforts effectively. For instance, while one team member might be driven by career advancement (aiming for a leadership role), another might value work-life balance more. Recognising these differences can help in assigning roles and responsibilities that align with individual motivations, enhancing overall productivity and satisfaction.

- **Promotes Empathy and Communication:**
  Realising that not everyone shares the same goals helps in developing empathy. It encourages individuals to engage in conversations that seek to understand and accommodate differing viewpoints and aspirations, which can lead to stronger, more meaningful relationships.

- **Reduces Conflict:**
  Many conflicts arise from misunderstandings or misaligned expectations. By acknowledging and discussing different goals openly, teams and individuals can negotiate and compromise more effectively, preventing conflicts and misunderstandings.

- **Facilitates Personal Growth:**
  When you acknowledge that others have different goals, it can also be a learning opportunity. Understanding why others may prioritise different outcomes can provide insights into other values and perspectives, which might influence or enhance your own goal-setting process.

- **Improves Management and Leadership:**
  For leaders and managers, understanding the diverse goals of their team members is essential for effective management. This understanding helps in motivating employees, designing better performance incentives, and fostering a workplace culture that values individual growth alongside organisational objectives.

In summary, realising that not everyone has the same goals as you is fundamental to creating an environment where individuals feel valued and understood. This recognition not only supports better teamwork and less conflict but also enriches the personal and professional growth of everyone involved.

Hindsight is a wonderful thing, as they say. The next few stories are from actual events and experiences of each of the group while they followed their own journey.

We'll start with the fewest: one of the group, Liam, did one, and that was the tandem jump. He loved the experience, but just never wanted to do it again. In fairness to him, he was and probably still is the most mature of all of us. Even at an early age he took off on the family route and had kids well before the rest of us. He is a wonderful guy, and I think he just saw his life was at a very different point than the rest of us, and he didn't want to continue the journey. His accomplishment was complete, he had achieved his own goal, and he didn't need or want to achieve anything further.

I had originally thought that he just wasn't interested in the heavy nights in the pub most weekends, but I may have been wrong. His cousin Conor had decided not to do any of the jumps at all – he thought it was absolute lunacy. He was a devote Christian, and I always used to say to him to convince him to do a jump that God would love to see him a little closer every now and then, but he was having none of it. 'God is always by my side', he would say. 'Fair enough, I suppose you'd probably have to pay for two slots each time to bring Him up there with you', would usually be my answer. A silly answer I know, but I thought it was funny.

Anyway, Conor used to drive a Ford Sierra and on a number of weekends, both he and Liam used to come to the club to watch us jump, join us in the pub that night, and spend the rest of the time joyriding around the small country roads at high-speed in the Sierra. I had been in that car many times, and although I said that I was more comfortable jumping out of the planes than staying in the plane to land again, this car was even worse. I'd have been too scared to join them – give me the skydiving any day. Each to their own, as they say, however, I do remember that we needed to rescue them from a ditch one weekend when they misjudged a bend in the road and went straight, leaving the road and joining the ditch. They both walked away with cuts and bruises – perhaps in hindsight it was better that both of them stayed on the ground.

Two of the other friends did two jumps each. Aidan did his solo jump first in the morning he arrived down, and the then did his tandem jump that afternoon – the very opposite order to how we did ours, and he said he thoroughly enjoyed them, but, and in his words, 'couldn't be arsed' to do any more.

Declan did two solo jumps and never did a tandem. His first jump was uneventful, and he came back another week to do another. He really enjoyed the nights out, but the actual activity of jumping from a plane, in his own words, 'scared the bejaysus' out of him.

On his second and last jump, when he was coming into land, he was listening very closely to what the instructor was saying on the radio in his ear. He was coming in a little fast, but not dangerously fast and into the wind as he should do, but there was little wind that day, so it didn't slow him down much. The instructor was very clear about the instructions and this guy was following them to a tee. We were all watching him as he came in to land, and with a final pull on both toggles, and flaring the parachute, his feet touched the ground. His momentum was still carrying him forward, but his feet remained planted in the ground. In an instant he was face down in the turf and being dragged down a field by the parachute.

Luckily there were a couple of seasoned skydivers on hand to catch him as he travelled across the field on his face.

As he walked back to us, with his newfound chaperones to either side, it became obvious that his face had thankfully received a soft landing, not just in the soft grass of the field, but straight into a freshly laid pile of sheep droppings. I don't think we have ever laughed as much as we did right then – this picture of a friend walking through a field, in a red jumpsuit, carrying a parachute accompanied by two experienced skydivers, who were trying to be supportive but were clearly holding back the laughter, and a face full of shite. And it wasn't just that picture that made it funny – it was the whole thing. The whole visual around the landing, and how it went and then seeing the expression on his face.

Generally, when you land you need to take a step to balance yourself, or perhaps a couple of steps, and it's just something that we do naturally. And when I say we all do it, that's not just referring to skydivers, it's referring to people in general – very few of us can make a jump at speed and land cleanly on two feet without taking an extra step – gymnasts spend years trying to perfect this – the rest of us don't. When we asked Declan what happened, all he said was, 'They never told me to take a step, so I didn't'.

He told us afterwards that he was so scared about the entire process that he feared doing anything other than exactly what he was told, and when he saw the ground coming up to him as he fell, he just said to himself, so be it and let it happen. I don't think I understand this approach, but I respect it. He never jumped again, and still to this day when I meet him for a pint, I can still see 'poo-face' in my head.

Now, Jack had all the fun in his 9-jump career. Jack is such a lovely guy, and it seems the gods were doing their best to bring him closer to them. But his time here was not over, despite their best efforts. From the main parachute failure on his very first jump, the tandem, to downwind landings, slipping off planes and cracking his elbow off the top of a sheep's head. (Did I mention that this place was the only place in the world where the sheep looked upwards?) Jack did his utmost to leave our world.

Jack was here for the craic, and that was it. If it meant he had to jump out of planes to continue with the craic, so be it. He's such a great people person, that even the thought of not being around the group would give him more fear that the act of skydiving itself. He once told me that he was terrified for every jump he did, and it never left him... 'shitting his bags' were the words he used, but he did more than the others and fair play to him. I often wonder that if the worst had happened, and he was looking down on us now, would he think, 'I don't know what I was thinking... those lads weren't that much craic, in fairness', but for Jack, it was the fear of missing out on something.

Leadership Lesson – The Fear Of Missing Out (FOMO)

The fear of missing out (FOMO) is a common psychological phenomenon where individuals feel anxious or stressed about potentially missing rewarding experiences others are having. When leaders experience FOMO, it can present several specific dangers to both their effectiveness and the health of their organisation:

- **Impulsive Decision-Making:**
  Leaders with FOMO may make hasty decisions without fully analysing the data or considering the long-term consequences. This is particularly risky in a business context where strategic decisions need careful planning and consideration. Seriously, I don't think Jack took

this into consideration when making his decisions to keep jumping, however, he does still walk among us, so risk avoided (luckily).

- **Lack of Focus:**
  FOMO can lead to a lack of focus on core goals and strategies. Leaders might chase after new trends, technologies or opportunities that seem promising without aligning them with the organisation's mission or strategic plan. This can divert resources and attention from more critical areas.

- **Overextension:**
  Trying to seize every opportunity can lead to spreading resources too thin. Overextension can exhaust teams and dilute the impact of their efforts, reducing overall productivity and potentially leading to burnout.

- **Neglected Team Morale and Trust:**
  Leaders who constantly shift focus and priorities can leave their teams feeling uncertain and undervalued. This can erode trust and morale, as team members may feel their efforts are wasted if the direction of their work keeps changing unpredictably.

- **Reduced Innovation:**
  While it might seem counterintuitive, too much emphasis on not missing out can actually stifle innovation. Teams may become more focused on catching up or keeping pace with competitors rather than developing unique and innovative solutions that provide real value.

- **Eroding Personal Well-being:**
  Leaders suffering from FOMO may find it difficult to disconnect or step back, which can lead to stress, anxiety, and even burnout. The pressure to be constantly involved and informed can take a toll on their mental and physical health.

- **Communication Breakdowns:**
  Constantly shifting goals and priorities can lead to confusion and ineffective communication within the team. If leaders are not clear and consistent, it can lead to misalignments and inefficiencies in how tasks are understood and executed.

To mitigate these dangers leaders need to develop a clear vision and stick to it, prioritise effectively, delegate when necessary, and take time to reflect on their decisions and the overall direction of their organisation. Building awareness about the implications of FOMO and actively managing its influence can help maintain a balanced, productive, and innovative leadership approach.

It's so important to be doing what you're doing for the right reasons. Don't become a leader just because you wish to hang out with other leaders (I shudder to think who would actually want to do that), or because you think that's what's expected of you. Run your own race. It took Jack 9 jumps to realise this – 9 jumps gave him plenty of opportunities for it all to go wrong. And if it went wrong, that's fine if you're there for the right reasons, but if you're just there for the 'craic', well what a waste that would be. Jack gave up after 9 jumps because he was there for all the wrong reasons – a very good decision.

Before I let Jack go I'd like to share with you the experience he had on his last jump where he fell off the plane. It just so happens that it was the same jump where he 'assaulted the sheep'.

Sometimes things move very fast at the drop zone. Because of the Irish weather there is so much time spent sitting around waiting for the clouds to clear or the rain to stop or the wind to stop blowing so strongly, so when the good weather comes in, it's all hands, the plane gets up to altitude as quickly as possible and back to ground even faster. On many occasions I remember gliding across the drop zone at two thousand feet and looking down to see the plane that I had just jumped from landed on the runway below me – not many people can say they've seen a plane landing from above.

On this occasion, as I was walking back to the hanger with my parachute in my hands, they were loading up the plane for its next flight and Jack was in the queue. He had forgotten his gloves and it was always cold up there. He shouted out to me to ask if he could borrow my gloves and I ran over to give them to him. You see, the thing about gloves in this setting is that they're not just there to keep your hands warm... they're used for grip too.

To cut a long story short, I had landed a little badly on that jump and I came to the ground on my arse, rather than 'delicately' landing on my feet. Whilst on my arse, I slid through many piles of sheep shit before coming to a stop, and whilst being thankful that I didn't nosedive into any of it like my friend had, my jumpsuit and gloves came off the worst for wear. While running to Jack looking like I'd just completed my first and only 'shite angel', I said, 'they're a bit messy mate', to which he replied, 'they'll be grand'.

Fast forward to Jack climbing out of the plane at 4,000 feet, wind in his face, one foot on the wheel, one hand on the strut, second hand on the strut, second foot on the wheel – time to dangle and wait to receive the cue to fall.

Sometimes, just dangling from the wing gives you a little time to compose yourself, which I always liked. It was just a couple of seconds, but for me, it felt so important to make sure you're in the right position and allowing the time for the instructor to see you off.

The moment Jack's feet came off the wheel, the sheep's shit on the gloves providing no grip at all caused Jack to just fall out into the sky without any warning. He just dropped, and the instructor just laughed and turned to the others in the plane and said, 'Shit, I didn't even have time to tell him to get the feck off – he's enthusiastic!!' While the instructor was saying this to the others in the plane, Jack's heart was in his mouth as he struggled to figure out what had just happened and cursed me from a height (literally speaking) for handing him a pair of gloves covered in shit. From my perspective, he knew what he was getting because I told him, and he could clearly see that the gloves weren't fit for purpose, however he still took them, because he was only thinking of how cold it was.

Leadership Lesson – Using the right tools

It's so important, especially as a leader, to ensure you have the right tools to hand (excuse the pun), and that the tools you use are suitable to all uses required.

Leaders ensuring that they use the right tools for the job and prepare for all eventualities, including running out of time, is crucial for several reasons:

- **Maximised Efficiency:**
  The right tools optimise productivity and efficiency, enabling teams to accomplish tasks more quickly and effectively. This becomes especially important when time constraints are tight. For example, using project management software can help allocate resources efficiently and prioritise tasks, which is critical when deadlines are approaching.

- **Quality Assurance:**
  High-quality outcomes are more likely when the appropriate tools are in use, even under time pressure. This means not just having the right technical tools, but also methodologies and frameworks that help

maintain standards of quality throughout the rush to completion. Also, they stop you falling from planes in some instances.

- **Risk Mitigation:**
  Being prepared for contingencies, including the possibility of running out of time, requires tools that offer flexibility and quick adaptation. Leaders need to anticipate potential problems and have plans in place to address them without delay. This could involve having backup systems, additional resources, alternative strategies ready to deploy, or clean gloves in your pocket.

- **Stress Reduction:**
  When leaders are prepared for time constraints and have the right tools at their disposal, it reduces stress for themselves and their teams. This preparation helps maintain morale and keeps teams focused and motivated, even in high-pressure situations.

- **Maintaining Reputation:**
  Leaders who can effectively manage time constraints and unforeseen challenges, thanks to proper preparation and the right tools, uphold and enhance their organisation's reputation. Successfully delivering on promises, particularly when obstacles arise, builds trust with clients and stakeholders.

- **Scalability and Future Preparedness:**
  Leaders who prepare for time limitations by choosing scalable and adaptable tools ensure that the organisation can grow without being hamstrung by initial setups. This forward-thinking approach means systems are already in place to handle increased demands, making future transitions smoother.

In summary, leaders who equip their teams with the right tools and prepare for every scenario, including time shortages, foster a resilient, proactive work culture. This not only ensures current project success but also sets a standard for future operations, enhancing overall organisational effectiveness.

Not that Jack really did, but don't blame others around you. It was not my fault that he used my gloves that day, it was his fault for forgetting his own and accepting mine in that state. There were many other options available to him, which also included going back to get his own gloves, but he cut a corner and borrowed my 'shitty' ones, ending up with a fairly 'shitty' experience because of that decision.

But it didn't matter, because that was that for Jack; that was his last jump. In a later chapter, I'll go through the journey of the remaining three, including myself who progressed into the freefall stages and further.

But first, the next chapter will ask you whether you can smell the farts... well, can you?

CHAPTER 10

CAN YOU SMELL THE FARTS YET?

I know, this is an unusual heading for a chapter, however, bear with me and I hope it makes sense to you soon.

While progressing through my skydiving training, an instructor asked me after the completion of approximately 5 jumps, 'Can you smell the farts yet?'

'What now? Did you...?' was my response, and he laughed, knowing that my surprise had already answered his question. So why would he ask such a question? Here's the scientific reason:

Flatulence at higher altitudes is primarily due to the decrease in atmospheric pressure. This phenomenon can be explained through Boyle's law, a fundamental principle in physics.

Boyle's law states that the pressure of a gas tends to decrease as the volume increases. At higher altitudes, the external atmospheric pressure is lower than it is at sea level. This lower pressure outside the body causes the gases inside the gastrointestinal tract to expand.

Inside the body gases are trapped in the gut as part of the digestive process, which includes swallowing air and the byproduct of the digestion of certain foods. At lower altitudes these gases are somewhat compressed due to the higher atmospheric pressure. When you ascend to a higher altitude the external pressure decreases, allowing the gas inside your intestines to expand. This expansion increases the volume of the gas and the body responds by expelling it, resulting in increased flatulence.

Additionally, changes in diet or eating habits, which often occur during travel to different altitudes or when engaging in activities like hiking, skydiving or flying, can also contribute to increased gas production in the digestive tract, further exacerbating the issue.

So, why did he ask? Although it may not be immediately apparent, as it certainly wasn't to me at the time, this question was meant to gauge my focus level.

Skydivers, especially those new to skydiving, are often in a heightened state of awareness due to adrenaline and fear. This heightened state can shift their focus away from less critical stimuli, like smells, to more important concerns, such as the upcoming jump. The psychological state of being focused and excited can temporarily make someone less sensitive to their surroundings, including odours.

As skydivers become more comfortable with the prospect of throwing themselves out of a perfectly good aircraft, their focus becomes more sensitive to the surroundings, and soon they are able to experience the odours that surround them. In a Cessna 206 which is a very small plane, in the company of a group of people who had consumed a silly amount of Guinness the night before, this odour was 'special', to say the least. In fact, at times, it encouraged you to get out of the plane as quickly as possible. So how does this relate to leadership?

Leadership Lesson – The Dangers of Complacency

Comparing the effects of complacency in skydiving to leading a team in business reveals some distinct parallels and differences. Complacency, defined as a self-satisfied lack of awareness about potential dangers or deficiencies, can have detrimental outcomes in both arenas, impacting safety, performance, and growth.

Skydiving

In skydiving complacency can lead to a direct, immediate threat to life and limb. The inherent risks of skydiving require strict adherence to safety protocols, equipment checks, and continuous learning and awareness of one's environment and conditions. The consequences of complacency here are stark:

- **Overlooked Safety Protocols:**
  Failing to meticulously check equipment or ignoring weather warnings due to overconfidence can lead to accidents.

- **Decreased Alertness:**
  Complacency may dull the skydiver's instinct for detecting and responding to unforeseen issues during the jump, such as sudden weather changes or equipment malfunction.

- **Catastrophic Outcomes:**
  The ultimate risk of complacency in skydiving is injury or death, starkly underscoring the need for vigilance at every step.

- **Leading a Team**
  Complacency in leading a team affects organisational dynamics, productivity, and the ability to achieve strategic goals. While the out-

comes may not be as immediately life-threatening as in skydiving, they can significantly undermine the health and success of a business:

- **Stagnation and Lack of Innovation:**
  Complacent leadership may result in a team that is resistant to change, limiting creativity and innovation. This can lead to the business being outpaced by more agile competitors.

- **Low Morale and Engagement:**
  A leader's complacency can trickle down to the team, resulting in disengagement and low morale. Without the drive for continuous improvement or new challenges, team members may lose their motivation.

- **Missed Opportunities and Declining Performance:**
  Complacency can blind leaders to emerging opportunities and threats, leading to poor decision-making and a decline in overall performance.

Comparisons and Contrasts

- **Scope and Scale of Impact:**
  While complacency in skydiving primarily endangers the individual involved, complacency in leadership affects the entire team and, by extension, the broader organisation and its stakeholders.

- **Nature of Consequences:**
  The consequences of complacency in skydiving are immediate and potentially fatal. In contrast, the effects in a business context unfold over time, eroding the team's effectiveness and competitive positioning.

- **Recovery and Correction:**
  Errors made due to complacency in skydiving may not allow for a second chance. However, in a business setting, there is typically the opportunity to recognise and correct course, though this may involve significant effort and resources to address ingrained complacency.

Despite these differences, the underlying threat of complacency in both scenarios highlights the universal importance of vigilance, continuous improvement, and an unyielding commitment to excellence. Whether navigating the skies or leading a team towards its goals, the antidote to complacency lies in fostering a culture that values awareness, challenges the status quo, and prioritises ongoing learning and development.

My instructor told me that this was when the accidents happened – as people became more comfortable with the task ahead of them, they sometimes disregarded or even sometimes forgot the fundamentals, and the consequences could be fatal. I've been reliably informed that across most clubs around the world, the accidents occur most frequently between 1,000 and 2,000 jumps.

The most interesting aspect of this form of questioning was the psychology behind the question. The way the question was asked distracted me from the core reason for the question, which was establishing my level of confidence. He didn't just ask if I was getting more confident, because in reality, I didn't know what confident looked like at this stage; I had only done a few jumps. He asked a question in a form that would allow me to provide an educated answer – I may not be an expert in jumping out of planes yet, but I can provide an educated answer about what I can smell.

By asking the question in this manner, he removed any opportunity for me to be dishonest with my answer, or to try to be stronger than I actually was or provide him with a false perspective on my current state. The question was set up so that the only answer I could provide was one based on fact and science. Was my body and brain getting more comfortable with the new levels of stress I was placing them under? The answer was Yes, and the answer to his question was also yes – I am now starting to smell the farts.

This unusual question and the reason it was asked like this was meant to ensure that the answer wasn't bluffed or lied about. It was phrased in a way that allowed only a truthful answer based purely on a person's senses, rather than their feelings. I was very impressed with the psychology of it and I wanted you - the reader - to easily recognise that there are different methods to achieve the right answer.

When we learn to drive, we are extremely attentive to the task at hand but as we continue to practice and drive more, we all know that bad habits start to emerge. We start speeding, we forget to use our seatbelts (although nowadays that annoying bell sounds until you 'clunk/click'), we ignore traffic signs thinking that surely they're not meant for me – I'm a good driver – we sit in the wrong lane, we tailgate or chat on the phone, we become enraged with other drivers (an action I could never understand) or sometimes, as we certainly did years ago in the parachute club, we drive whilst under the influence of alcohol.

As we become better and more competent at something we start to cut corners and become overconfident in our abilities. We disregard or forget the fundamentals and believe 'nothing will happen to me'. Why? Because 'I'm a good driver'.

Does it sound like you're a good driver? If this was the way you completed your tasks in the work environment, you would either be in the middle of a performance improvement plan or in the middle of a queue in the job centre.

I wonder how many of us would pass our driving test now using the same driving methods we so callously employ on the road.

Most of this behaviour is driven (excuse the pun) on the belief that we are better than we really are.

Leadership Lesson – The Dangers of Overconfidence

Overconfidence often lays the groundwork for complacency by fostering a false sense of security and an underestimation of risks, challenges, or the need for improvement. This dynamic can manifest in various contexts, from individual activities and professions to leadership and team dynamics in business. Here's how overconfidence contributes to complacency:

Misjudgement of Risk and Abilities

Overconfidence can lead individuals to believe they are less vulnerable to the risks and challenges that may befall others, leading to a dangerous underestimation of the complexities or dangers involved in a situation.

Neglect of Continuous Improvement

An overconfident mindset often comes with the belief that one's skills, knowledge, or strategies are already at their peak, reducing the perceived need for further learning or adaptation. This can halt personal and professional growth, as individuals and organisations fail to update their practices or expand their knowledge base. In rapidly evolving fields, such as technology or global markets, this stagnation can quickly lead to obsolescence.

Reduced Vigilance

Overconfidence can dull an individual's vigilance, both in physical activities like sports or high-risk endeavours, and in cognitive tasks such as strategic planning or problem-solving in business. The assumption that one is fully prepared or that situations are fully understood can lead to overlooking critical details, misinterpreting data, or failing to anticipate changes, each of which can have severe consequences in terms of safety, efficiency, and effectiveness.

Weakening of Feedback Loops

Constructive feedback is crucial for improvement and risk management. However, overconfident individuals or teams may discount negative feedback or external advice, believing their methods or strategies are beyond reproach. This not only solidifies complacency but also isolates them from valuable insights and learning opportunities that could prevent future failures or mishaps.

The Illusion of Control

Overconfidence often creates an illusion of control over external events, leading individuals to overestimate their ability to influence outcomes. This misperception can discourage proper preparation and risk assessment, as the individual or team assumes they can manage any situation regardless of preparation levels or external variables.

In essence, overconfidence acts as a catalyst for complacency by creating a false sense of security, discouraging the pursuit of improvement, and undermining the mechanisms of learning and adaptation that are essential for success and safety in any endeavour. Recognising and mitigating overconfidence is therefore crucial to avoiding the pitfalls of complacency.

Not only could I smell the farts now, I was getting a little cocky and the instructor could see this. I had only completed 5 jumps at this stage, and my confidence was coming from the fact that I had done that many, the fact that it had taken me so long to do 'that many', purely from the poor weather and long weekends sitting in the club looking up at the rain clouds, the fact that I felt I had so much more experience because I had been at the club for so long (I hadn't really), the fact that everyone kept telling me how well I was doing, and the fact that on my previous jump, when I had been taken off the radio for the first time, received a 'bum' spot and made it back to the drop zone, well nearly, on my own.

Relatively speaking, I knew nothing at this stage, but the fear was leaving me and the confidence was setting in, and I needed a kick in the backside... that's why he asked, 'Can you smell the farts yet?'

This was always when the mistakes happened, and in hindsight, it was the right time to check in with me. I was already doing stupid things on the periphery of skydiving, such as climbing onto car roofs whilst travelling at speed and getting quite drunk the night before and hiding it from the instructors. There were mornings that I would arrive at the drop zone with possibly 2 hours sleep the night before. On one occasion I never left the drop zone from the night before and I slept under a tree in a field halfway down the runway – don't ask... I have no idea.

The management of the club was extremely strict when it came to safety, and they were very clear about not allowing people into the aircraft if they suspected that someone was under the influence of alcohol, either drinking on the day of a jump, which some people had tried to do to calm their nerves, but also the morning after a big night.

During this time in Ireland, there was never any talk about being impaired the morning after a big night out. Back in those days, if the Gardai pulled you over while driving a car and expected that you had to much drink, rather than do the paperwork they would usually tell you to park up the car and walk home.

It's only in the last 10 or 15 years that the Irish government has cracked down on drink driving, and now has a zero tolerance for it. And that includes the morning after. So many people over the last few years have been pulled over the morning after a night out and lost their licences, and rightly so, because their blood alcohol levels were still over the limit.

We all know this, and we always have done, but it took the enforcement of rules and regulations to ensure we stopped this behaviour to keep our roads safe. It's the same in business and whilst leading a team.

Human behaviour is as it is, and whilst some people have the moral compass to guide them through decision making, others do not, and need strict guidelines to help them understand. We knew the consequences of being under the influence of alcohol while skydiving, and despite it being extremely detrimental to our health, the reason we did our best to ensure we were sober enough to jump was so they would allow us to, and not for the most obvious reason, to ensure we stayed alive. It's the same for a lot of people who don't drink and drive... they don't because they wish to continue to drive and don't want to go to prison. In a lot of cases the thoughts of causing harm to yourself, or to others, is unfortunately ranked below a number of other factors on the priority list.

This is just human behaviour and it's so important to understand that people do not necessarily intend to cut corners or break rules, sometimes they just don't either know them or understand the need for them. It's so important, as mentioned previously. that people know the rules from the outset, know the consequences of breaking those rules, and most importantly understand the reasoning behind those rules. We all know that we shouldn't drink and drive, and we all know the reasoning behind those rules, yet some people still do it, therefore the enforcement is so important; not enforcing these rules can allow the negative behaviours to creep back in.

Leadership Lesson – Enforcement of Rules

Enforcing rules and regulations is crucial for a leader for several reasons, each contributing to the effective management and success of any organisation or community:

- **Maintaining Order and Discipline:**
  Rules and regulations are foundational to maintaining order and discipline within an organisation. When leaders enforce these consistently, it helps ensure that operations run smoothly and efficiently. This consistency also helps in preventing chaos and mitigating conflicts that can arise from ambiguities or misunderstandings about acceptable behaviour.

- **Upholding Integrity and Ethics:**
  By enforcing rules, leaders set a standard of integrity and ethics. This is particularly important in setting a moral compass for the organisation and for modelling behaviour for employees or followers. Leaders who actively uphold these standards encourage a culture of honesty and trust, which are critical for long-term success.

- **Ensuring Fairness and Equality:**
  Fair enforcement of rules and regulations ensures that all members of an organisation are treated equally. This fosters a sense of fairness and justice within the group, which can enhance morale and loyalty. It also helps prevent discrimination and biases, ensuring that decisions are made based on merit and defined standards rather than personal preferences or nepotism.

- **Promoting Accountability:**
  When leaders enforce rules, they promote a culture of accountability. Members of the organisation learn that there are consequences for

their actions. This accountability extends upwards as well, as leaders must also adhere to the same standards they set for others, thereby reinforcing their legitimacy and authority.

- **Facilitating Improvement and Adaptation:**
  Effective enforcement of rules doesn't just involve adhering to existing norms but also includes evaluating and adapting those rules as necessary. A leader who is in tune with the needs of their organisation and its external environment can facilitate improvements to rules and processes, promoting innovation and ensuring the organisation remains relevant and competitive.

- **Building Trust and Credibility:**
  Leaders who consistently enforce rules and follow them themselves are more likely to be viewed as credible and trustworthy. This trust is crucial not only for internal management but also in the eyes of external stakeholders, such as partners, customers, and regulatory bodies.

- **Protecting the Organisation:**
  Rules often exist to protect the organisation from risks, including legal risks, financial penalties, and reputational damage. Leaders who effectively enforce these regulations protect the organisation from potential external threats and internal vulnerabilities.

Overall, the enforcement of rules and regulations by leaders is not merely about maintaining control but about fostering a healthy, ethical, and productive environment. It reflects a commitment to the values and objectives of the organisation and is vital for its stability and growth.

My friend Sean had multiple run-ins with the club's management for this very reason. He would never ever think about jumping on a day that he was drinking, but he was dreadful the morning after a night before. Sean is about 6 foot 3 inches and not a pick on him, which means he's quite slender. I've known Sean since I was seven years old. (Remember the whole 1970's one eyed teddy bear swap fiasco? That was Sean). Before we started this journey Sean and I had an excellent arrangement to make the most out of our cashflow. Sean spent most of his younger adult days as an employee of the state, or in other words, unemployed. This was his choice, and he enjoyed a life of leisure. We both lived at home and all we needed money for was to go out at night and enjoy ourselves – wow, how simple things were back then. I would get paid from my job on a Thursday, and I would lend him money that he could spend from a Thursday to a Sunday night. Then on Mondays, I would always be broke, so when Sean collected his social welfare payment, he would pay me back, and both of us would have a little bit of money to keep us going until Thursday came around again and the circle started again. I remember Sean once saying, or rather singing to me on a Thursday after I got paid, 'We're in the money, we're in the money'. In fact, I think he used to sing this every week, but never mind. It always made me laugh that he used to view his social welfare payment as sustenance, and my weekly wage as something to celebrate. We often thought that all we had to do was miss one weekend of going out and we would break the circle, but that never happened.

Sean was never a great person for holding his drink and sometimes he would spend an entire day in bed the day after a night out. I was a little heavier, or probably a lot heavier, and could hold it a little better – I possibly had a little more resources available to me to soak up the alcohol than Sean had, and due to having a job I had to hold down, I was able to get myself out of bed in the morning, shake it off and get to work. Sean's job as a state employee provided him with a little more flexibility than I had to allow him to take a longer and more relaxed way of curing the hangover.

It wasn't until we took up skydiving, and the requirement to get up bright and early every morning after the night before to get in line for our jumps, that the tolerance I had built up over the years showed its usefulness. For Sean it was quite the opposite, and on so many occasions, he would get sent back to the B&B to sleep it off, which obviously meant that he missed quite a number of opportunities to jump, and it slowed down his progression. I remember as the club's management got to know Sean a little better, sometimes he wouldn't get within 50 yards of them, and the Skydive Manifest, the person who coordinated and planned the day's events on behalf of the club (such a funny and great guy – I'll never forget him) would call out on the loudspeaker, 'Back home to bed Sean, I can see you wobbling from here – see you after lunch' – and off Sean would go, and back to bed. When he got back to the drop zone he'd be in good shape to jump, but sometimes the queue would be too long at that stage, or the weather would have changed, and he would on many occasions return back to Dublin without even doing one jump.

To be honest, I probably knew that I wasn't in great shape these mornings, but I didn't allow it to stop me, and I managed to hide it from the club. I wanted to progress as fast as I could, and whilst I ensured that I performed each of my jumps exactly how they should be, I probably could have done better and with a lot more ease if I had a clearer head on my shoulders. Either way, I was successful in hiding this from the club and was never sent back home to sleep it off. In hindsight, how irresponsible was this? I was placing the speed of my progression ahead of my own safety and wellbeing.

Leadership Lesson – Lead by Example & Look after Yourself

A lot of times in leadership it's easy to get caught up in the same way.

We tell our teams to ensure that they take their allotted time for lunch yet we sit at our desks eating a sandwich while we work. And the reason we do this is to progress quickly up the ladder. We place progression ahead of safety and wellbeing.

Leaders, like anyone else, can fall into the trap of 'do as I say, not as I do'. Here are some common mistakes that leaders might caution their staff against, yet occasionally make themselves:

- **Micromanaging:**
  Leaders often advise their teams to empower subordinates and delegate tasks effectively. However they sometimes fail to practice this themselves, especially under pressure, feeling the need to control every detail, which can stifle team autonomy and innovation. We need to trust our team especially in times of pressure. Falling back into micromanagement especially in a time of pressure is counter intuitive and results in less productivity.

- **Poor Communication:**
  Leaders typically stress the importance of clear and open communication and expect it from their team. Yet, they might not always model this behaviour effectively. They might not share enough information, provide inconsistent messages, or fail to listen actively to their teams' concerns and feedback. We're all human, but we need to be self-aware enough to notice the times that we may slip backwards.

- **Resisting Change:**
  Leaders might encourage their staff to be adaptable and embrace new challenges and changes. However, leaders themselves can sometimes be resistant to change due to comfort with the status quo or fear of the unknown, which can hinder organisational growth.

- **Failing to Learn from Mistakes:**
  While leaders often promote a culture of seeing failures as learning opportunities, they might not always openly acknowledge or learn from their own mistakes. This can create a discrepancy between what they preach and what they practice, potentially leading to a lack of trust and respect. Never be concerned about apologising for mistakes and learning from them. Failure is a part of the process of success – without failure, and acceptance of same, leaders would never learn and grow.

- **Not Taking Responsibility:**
  Leaders expect their team members to take responsibility for their actions, but sometimes leaders might shift the blame to others or external circumstances when things go wrong under their watch. This is more common than not, and unfortunately there are too many leaders who adopt a blame culture within their teams. Someone once said to me, 'If you are pointing the finger at someone else, the remaining fingers on your hand are pointing at the true culprit'. And this is so true. As a leader, and if you wish to be an accountable leader, everything is your fault, and you need to look deeply within yourself to see if you could have done something differently to prevent this mistake from happening.

The most effective leaders are those who prevent mistakes from happening. This is not always possible, but effective leaders can identify and forecast the possibility of something going wrong from every possible action. Always ask yourself when making a decision,

'What's the worst that can happen?' and then mitigate the risk. If you believe that the risk is worth it, take the action – but if it goes wrong, also take the ownership of it, because you damn sure would have taken the credit if it went well.

- **Neglecting Self-Care:**
  Leaders often emphasize the importance of work-life balance, mental health, and self-care to their staff but might neglect their own. This can lead to burnout and decreased effectiveness as a leader. I am a perfect example of this, and I always have been. I know that I do this, and yet I still do it. When asked in an interview about my weaknesses, this is always it. I mitigate against it because I delegate well, and I ensure I don't have too much on my own personal plate at any one time to risk burnout. As a rule, I never fill my plate and always allow room for, well, 'What's the worst that can happen?' The worst that can happen in this scenario is that my plate was already too full when something went wrong, and during the chaos, as more and more gets lumped onto my plate, the plate overflows and I start to spill my food. And when your plate is too full and you start spilling your food, you usually leave a mess that somebody else needs to clean up. Always leave space for the unexpected.

- **Overlooking Professional Development:**
  Leaders might encourage their staff to pursue continuous learning and professional development. However, they can sometimes become so wrapped up in their managerial duties that they don't take time for their own development, potentially falling behind in latest industry practices. A key part of leadership is continuous learning. When completing your targets, or goals each year, always ensure that you, and your team include personal development goals.

Leaders being aware of these common pitfalls and actively working to avoid them can significantly enhance their credibility and effectiveness. It fosters a healthier, more productive work environment where the principles promoted are visibly practiced at all levels, starting at the top.

The more confident you become in your role, either as a leader or as a skydiver, the easier it becomes to forget the fundamentals. No matter how long you've been leading teams, people are always watching you, and sometimes the slightest mistakes can push you back years. You need to be perfect all of the time and that's not possible, right? Yeah, your right, it's not. None of us are perfect, but we have to accept that and sometimes when we make mistakes, it's how we deal with them and manage ourselves through these times that makes us perfect in our own way. Nobody expects leaders to be perfect, but they are expected to be as perfect as possible, and being authentic in owning your mistakes is key to maintaining trust and respect. In skydiving, there is no escape from perfection, because there is no way to apologise after a potentially fatal mistake. There is no way back.

Leaders often strive for perfection in an attempt to set high standards and serve as a role model for their teams. While the drive for excellence can have positive effects, putting too much pressure on oneself to be perfect can also have significant drawbacks. Here's a look at the pros and cons of this approach, and please note that there are more cons, than pros:

Pros

- **High Standards:**
  Aiming for perfection can lead to high standards of work, which can drive quality improvements across the organisation. It encourages a culture of excellence where good enough is never enough, potentially leading to superior outcomes.

- **Role Modelling:**
  By striving for perfection, leaders can demonstrate their commitment to excellence. This can inspire employees to emulate these high standards in their own work, fostering a motivated and ambitious workforce.

- **Attention to Detail:**
  Perfectionist leaders often pay close attention to details that might be overlooked by others. This can help in catching errors and ensuring that the organisation's outputs are of the highest quality.

Cons

- **Unrealistic Expectations:**
  Constantly aiming for perfection might set unrealistic standards that are impossible to meet. This can lead to frustration and dissatisfaction for both the leader and their team members, who may feel they are never able to 'measure up.' As a result, they may no longer give their all because it's not recognised or appreciated. This can also result in high employee turnover.

- **Risk Aversion:**
  Perfectionism can lead to a fear of failure, where leaders might avoid taking risks that could potentially lead to mistakes. This risk aversion can stifle innovation and creativity, which are essential for growth and adaptation in dynamic environments.

- **Work-Life Balance Issues (my personal blind-spot):**
  Leaders who pressure themselves to be perfect may work excessively long hours and expect the same from their team. This can harm personal and team morale and lead to burnout, reducing overall productivity and job satisfaction.

- **Impeding Team Development:**
  Leaders who focus too much on perfection might micromanage, believing they are the only ones who can perform tasks to the necessary standard. This can stifle creativity and innovation and limit opportunities for team members to develop skills and take ownership, potentially leading to disengagement and a lack of initiative among team members.

- **Delayed Decision-Making:**
  Perfectionist leaders might delay decisions, waiting for the perfect solution. In fast-paced environments, this can lead to missed opportunities and can hinder the organisation's ability to respond swiftly to market changes.

- **High Stress Levels:**
  The stress of striving to be perfect can be overwhelming and detrimental to the leader's mental and physical health. Chronic stress can impair decision-making and leadership effectiveness.

While striving for perfection can elevate a leader's performance and influence within an organisation, it's important for leaders to recognise the balance between pursuing excellence and the realistic limits of their roles and personal health. Embracing a mindset that focuses on continuous improvement rather than perfection can alleviate some of the pressures and lead to more sustainable leadership practices. Take the pressure off yourself and live a little.

Perfection in skydiving is so important, and instructors micromanaged us to ensure that we did everything correctly. In this world, micromanagement is not a bad word, and it is gratefully accepted by the participants. When I was asked if I could smell the farts yet, the instructor was relying on the honesty of my response; but it was designed to intentionally confuse me. For me, that question didn't appear to have any underlying meaning to it, so there was no reason for me to attempt to give a dishonest response. I didn't know the context and the reason for asking this question. Now, if the question had been, 'Do you think you're getting a bit too big for your boots right now?' I believe my answer would have been a different one, and possibly a more defensive answer. I think I would have said, 'Absolutely not', which would have been untrue. The instructors understand the psychology of human behaviour and have adapted their questioning in an unusual manner, however a very effective manner to ensure they achieve a truthful response. This is also very important in leadership, and phrasing your questions appropriately can ensure you also receive the truthful answers from your team.

My instructor brought me back to ground and revisited the fundamentals of skydiving with me again. He re-emphasised the serious nature of the sport, providing me with very clear and honest feedback, and also praising me for the things I was doing well. He was very clear however that I was a 'newbie', and that I knew nothing about the sport as yet, but he said, with the right attitude and a good head on your shoulders, 'You'll do well at this, and you'll continue to live another day after each jump'.

One of our friends, who was nicknamed 'Dead Man Walking' had a near fatal accident which we'll discuss shortly, and after that happened, I asked him if he had ever been asked about the 'farts', and he said he hadn't. We believe to this day that because we were all seen as the one group and because a number of us appeared to be progressing at the same speed, that Sean may have slipped through the cracks because of the number of times he was sent home to sleep off the hangover. The perception of the instructors of the team was that Sean had been there as long as the rest of us, and was progressing through his jumps, that someone must have had the conversation with him. Someone must have pulled him aside to check in with him, but nobody had. They would definitely have done so had they known, but for some reason, he just slipped through the cracks.

Sean could smell the farts, and was taking chances that none of us knew about until it was too late.

CHAPTER 11

MY EXPERIENCE

And then there were three of us. And all three of us wanted to be the first to freefall. Although we were all great friends, we never thought about how great it would be to share the moment together, we just wanted to beat each other.

Before I go into detail about Sean and Kieran, this is my experience from when I started my solo, or static line, journey to replicate that tandem jump I had done in 1994 and then again in 1998.

As with the rest of my friends, we signed up for this journey almost immediately after we all had completed our tandem jumps. We didn't manage to do them all on the same weekend, so we obviously had to thoroughly discuss each of our jumps in the pub at home every chance we got.

We were seriously painful to anyone else within earshot around us – there was nothing else we would speak about. We were so caught up in the experience that people would give us a wide berth when we came into our local pub. It was the same throughout the entire journey, until just 3 of us were left, and then the topic of conversations would expand past the skies and back into real life again.

As I remember back, there were times, and I joke not, that the whole group of us would be sitting in the pub, someone would say 'Arch' (the position required to stabilise yourself when exiting the plane) and the whole lot of us would throw our hands in the air and count, 'One one thousand, two one thousand, three one thousand'. For us, it was great fun – we were all in that place together and we were loving every moment of it. All except one friend Conor who just couldn't have been bothered doing this. Maybe he was embarrassed or thought it was childish. I don't know. He had to sit there amongst us and was the only person not raising their hands. He did it once just to be a part of the action but he was jokingly ridiculed with obvious put downs and he never did it again. But we're all still friends. Funnily enough, he was the only one of us who didn't drink Guinness. Maybe that was the thing, but probably not. We would order a round of drinks, and, somewhat like the lyric in Christy Moore's song, Lisdoonvarna:

"Before the Chieftains could start to play,
Seven creamy pints came out on a tray".

Seven creamy pints would come out on a tray to us, and one pint of lager for our friend. We would usually order '7 pints please, and a pint of bravery for our friend here'.

In all fairness, we were the assholes, not him. I can only imagine the other people in the pub watching us. Only recently I told some people who I knew back then, and still know now, that I was writing this book and they instantly agreed when I said that we behaved like a bunch of assholes. The smile of relief appeared on their faces knowing that I had finally realised what they had known for years but never would say because, well, they were polite. For the others in the pub, every time we did what must have looked like a ridiculous 'Mexican wave', I can only imagine what they thought. If that was today, we'd be on everyone's TikTok with some very distasteful comments, and rightly so.

But it's funny how people behave around you at these times. We made new friends who loved the enjoyment of the journey we were on. These friends would come to the club with us, would join all the parties, would hang on every word. They would never jump, but they just wanted to be involved. Our other friends, our true friends, took a subtle step back. Our good friend, you know, the 'pint of brave', he took a significant step back and always had an excuse when we were going out as a group. He would meet us individually, but never as a group, and looking back, I don't blame him at all. Since all of this nonsense stopped, we have all grown closer again, and it's never really spoken about these days. All of our conversations are back to discussing real life and nothing is mentioned about this 'bubble' we used to live in.

And I hear you ask: what about all the new friends? Where are they? The answer is, God only knows. Once the journeys came to an end, these friends flittered away almost as quickly as they'd flittered in. When I look back, it almost scares me how I may have jeopardised the strong relationships I'd had with long term friends, for the fleeting attention of some 'passers-by'.

Leadership Lesson – Building & Maintaining Healthy Relationships

This phenomenon is a common challenge for leaders across various fields, whether in business, politics, or community organisations.

Here are some key challenges leaders face in this context:

- **Authentic Relationships:**
  Leaders often struggle to discern whether friendships and interactions are genuine or if they are driven by their position and the power it holds. This can lead to a sense of isolation and scepticism, complicating personal connections.

- **Manipulation Risks:**
  There is a risk that individuals may befriend leaders solely to gain favour or influence decisions, which can lead to manipulation. Leaders need to be vigilant and perceptive to differentiate between true interest and ulterior motives.

- **Loneliness at the Top:**
  The phrase, 'it's lonely at the top', captures the isolation leaders can feel when they are unable to form authentic relationships due to their role. This loneliness can impact their mental health and overall well-being.

- **Pressure to Conform:**
  Leaders may feel pressure to fit a certain image or role expected by others, which can stifle their authentic selves. This pressure can be exhausting and demoralizing, leading to burnout.

- **Trust Issues:**
  Leaders may develop trust issues if they repeatedly encounter situations where their role, rather than their personality or effectiveness in the workplace, attracts people. Building trust becomes a strategic decision rather than a natural process, complicating both professional and personal interactions.

- **Balancing Professionalism and Friendship:**
  Leaders need to navigate the fine line between maintaining professionalism in workplace relationships and being approachable and personable. Finding this balance can be challenging and can affect team dynamics and leadership effectiveness. As a leader you're not there to make friends but you also don't want to alienate people.

To address these challenges leaders can benefit from developing strong self-awareness, seeking genuine connections outside of their professional role, and establishing clear boundaries between personal and professional interactions. They can also engage in mentoring or peer support groups with other leaders who face similar issues, providing a safe space to discuss and manage these unique challenges.

All I can say is to be careful of the people who surround you when you assume a position of authority. Although it is slightly different to why these 'passers-by' surrounded us, and it was definitely fun having them around, it was a fleeting encounter that only served to provide me with some personal self-confidence. Once the reason for their stay was no longer there, they were gone. Thankfully, my relationship with my other friends was so strong that it didn't have a lasting effect, however in business it could. I did need to apologise though, and rightly so. Never be afraid to apologise if you get something wrong – it's not a sign of weakness... it's very much a sign of strength. Those who believe it to be a weakness are those who you should distance yourself from.

Anyway, back to my journey.

My first solo jump was from 3,000 feet and was so much fun. Nothing exciting happened and all went as it should. I have to be honest that although I had previously done 2 tandem jumps, there was a comfort in the fact that a man was strapped to my back – possibly the only time in my life that I could confidently use that statement – and that he was in charge of everything if something should go wrong. This was very different, and although the parachute would open without my input as it was a static line jump, and all I had to do was literally fall out of a plane, there was the added pressure of 'what if the parachute doesn't open'... 'will I remember my training'... 'how do I recognise a bad opening and what if I cut away a perfectly good canopy and then the reserve doesn't open'... and what if, and what if, and what if. I could finish this book with all the 'what if's' because there were so many going through my head.

There were 5 of us in the little Cessna 182, the pilot, the instructor and 3 static line jumpers, or trainees, including me. I was first in line and to be honest, I can't remember who the other trainees were, and no matter how hard I try, I still can't remember. Your mind is awash with some many thoughts and none of them are positive – every one of them is about all of the things that could go wrong, and seriously, how stupid an idea this was in the first place – seriously, I don't belong here doing this, what if it all goes wrong and I forget everything I've been taught – what if this is the last time I see my friends and family and for what... for what? Why did I put myself in this position and was I really ready for it?

These are all the questions I remember asking myself when I started in my first role of leadership – albeit slightly different, but the hesitance in my confidence was the same.

Leadership Lesson – Confidence

First-time leaders often face a range of worries and concerns when they start leading a team. These can include:

- **Imposter Syndrome:**
  Many new leaders feel like they don't deserve their role or are not qualified enough, which can lead to self-doubt and anxiety.

- **Decision-Making:**
  The pressure of making decisions that will affect the whole team can be daunting, especially when those decisions are complex or have significant consequences.

- **Conflict Resolution:**
  Handling conflicts within the team can be challenging for first-time leaders. You may not quite be 'accepted' yet so there is no trust factor

you can rely on. It requires a balanced approach to address different personalities (with which you are not yet familiar) and issues effectively.

- **Team Dynamics:**
  Understanding and managing the dynamics of a new team, including building trust, fostering collaboration, and motivating team members, are critical challenges for new leaders.

- **Communication Skills:**
  Effective communication is crucial, and many new leaders worry about their ability to clearly and effectively convey their vision, provide feedback, and address team concerns.

- **Delegation:**
  Learning to delegate effectively can be difficult. New leaders often struggle with either micromanaging tasks or delegating too much without appropriate oversight.

- **Performance Management:**
  Evaluating team members' performances and providing constructive feedback, while also managing underperformance, can be particularly stressful.

- **Leadership Style:**
  Developing a personal leadership style that is effective and resonates with team members is often a concern. New leaders may experiment with different styles before finding what works best for them and their team.

- **Professional Growth:**
  Concerns about their own development, how to seek mentorship, and finding resources to improve their leadership skills are common among new leaders.

- **Balancing Roles:**
  Transitioning from a team member to a leader can complicate relationships with former peers and requires adjustments in social dynamics at work.

Addressing these concerns typically involves seeking mentorship, engaging in leadership training, and gaining practical experience with the support of more seasoned leaders. Support is likely the most important link in successfully transitioning into a new leadership role. I didn't receive support when I first became a leader and it really felt like I was freefalling without a parachute, without anyone to catch me. Having a supportive culture around you is so important to help you feel confident and help you pick up the pieces when something goes wrong, because it will. Preparing to fail is just a part of the process of becoming a leader – it's not a failure... it's a learning opportunity. And yes, I get it that it sometimes doesn't feel like that, but in the right company of supportive people, it will. If you're not in that environment, that's also a learning, and perhaps it'll teach you to leave that environment and go somewhere that will appreciate your humanity and not have unrealistic expectations of you.

'What if it all goes wrong?' I heard my instructor shouting at me over the sound of the engines: 'What if you forget your training?' He was reading my mind – how was he doing that? What kind of crazy mind-reading lunatic is shouting at me right now? He had already opened the door, and he was lying on the floor of the plane looking down trying to find the spot'. This was to find the most suitable place for 'the jumpers to exit the plane considering wind and other variables which would give them the best opportunity to land safely back at the drop zone. This guy had his head out of a plane looking down at the ground, and when you're afraid of heights, that's the one thing you're told not to do. But there he was, cool as a cucumber, head out of the plane and shouting at me with the exact same questions that were going through my head.

He was crazy, but he wasn't a mind-reading crazy lunatic – he'd just been where I was before, and many jumps ago. He knew exactly what was going through my mind and he knew that I needed support. 'You've nothing to worry about Dara – we've got you and you'll be great'. And just as he said that, a voice in my ear said, 'And we've got you too buddy'. It was one of the instructors on the ground through the radio earpiece. 'We'll tell you if you need to cut away, so don't worry about that, and we'll get you back to the drop zone... just think about the pints you'll buy us later in the pub'.

The instructor in the plane just looked at me and said, 'You good?' I gave a thumbs up; he turned to the pilot and told him to cut the engines and then there was silence. The plane started to glide and I needed to move fast. 'Out you go Dara – you know what to do', he said as he held my arm. I placed one leg onto the top of the wheel, I reached one hand out onto the strut of the wing right on top of the blue handprints (with five fingers on each handprint at this time) and then the other hand and all that was left was my other leg. I brought that out onto the wheel, looked down, thought to myself, 'Oh shit', and then I dangled for what felt like an eternity. I could feel my grip loosening as the plane glided at a speed of about 70 miles per hour and although I was just about to jump, I didn't want to 'slip and fall'. My legs dangled behind me as I was being pulled along by the plane and my training taught me to just turn my head towards the door of the plane and wait for the instructor to give me the signal.

At this stage, there is no way back. If you don't let go when the instructor tells you to, and if you have the strength to maintain your grip, which I certainly did not because it wasn't easy, the instructor will step out of the plane and pull your hands off the strut – it's that simple. But even in this precarious position, I still felt safer than letting go, however that wasn't going to stop me now. If I was going to quit, I had missed that moment. Funnily, thinking back, I think I was so worried about what could go wrong with the jump that I never even once thought about not doing it, and as the time approached, the distraction provided by the instructors both in the plane and on the ground ensured that it didn't cross my mind at all.

I looked into the door of the plane and the instructor gave me the thumbs up. I released my grip and fell into the sky. We needed to complete our count, so I called out, 'One one thousand, two one thousand, three one thousand', and as I did, the parachute was opening. It wasn't as swift of an opening as I'd experienced during the tandem jumps purely because I wasn't falling at the speed that I had been when doing those jumps – I would need to be falling for a longer period for that – I had probably only fallen 300 feet at this stage so I hadn't reached full speed, or maximum velocity as they call it.

I performed all of my checks that I'd learned from my training - it all came back to me instantly – and as I was releasing my toggles, the radio in my ear said, 'Looking good buddy'. I do believe this instructor knew my name, whether he remembered it not, or it was written on a piece of paper for him, but he was a 'buddy' kind of guy. You know the people who always call you 'buddy' or 'pal'. I only do that when I genuinely can't remember someone's name, but he did it for everyone, and that was ok with me. To be honest, I felt like I was his buddy while he was talking me down through the sky. My descent was unforgettable. The peace and tranquillity were incomparable, if of course you can get over the fact that you're attached to a harness hanging from a large piece of cloth over 2,500 feet in the air and totally on your own. I got over it quickly and loved every minute of it. It is the only place that I have truly ever experienced silence and serenity and, except for the words in my ear issuing instructions from the ground, it was beautiful. In later jumps I wouldn't need the radio, but for this jump and a couple more, I did, and it was more than welcome. I remember thinking that I couldn't even hear the noise of the cars as I saw them on the ground below. Unless you have experienced a jump, I don't think you'll ever understand this feeling. The feeling of calmness, despite the unusual environment I found myself in, was overwhelming.

I ended up experiencing this feeling so many times, but I think you'll always remember the first time, and although the previous couple of canopy rides I'd had were in the company of that man attached to my back, this was different.

In times of crisis I return to this place. I am often also accused of bringing others to this place with me, as when something happens in the world of leadership, and people are panicking all around, being able to transport yourself to a calm and serene place is so important. And I know I sound like Pheobe from Friends when I say this, but you've got to find your own 'happy place' – and I had found mine.

Here's a picture of my first solo landing – don't I look happy?

Leadership Lesson – Remaining Calm in a Crisis (part 2)

Remaining calm as a leader during a crisis is crucial for several reasons:

- **Decision Making:**
  Calmness aids in clear thinking and better decision-making. During a crisis, decisions often need to be made quickly and under pressure. A calm leader can assess situations more objectively without letting emotions cloud judgment.

- **Inspiring Confidence:**
  Leaders set the tone for their organisations. If a leader remains calm, it inspires confidence and can help stabilise the team's morale, preventing panic and fostering a sense of security among team members.

- **Effective Communication:**
  Calm leaders communicate more effectively. During a crisis, clear and concise communication is essential to ensure that everyone understands their roles and responsibilities and the steps needed to manage the situation.

- **Maintaining Focus:**
  By staying calm, leaders can maintain focus on the most critical tasks without getting overwhelmed by the situation. This focus helps in prioritising actions that are most beneficial for managing the crisis.

Here are some tips for maintaining calm as a leader during a crisis:

- **Prepare in Advance:**
  Anticipate potential crises and prepare for them. Having a crisis management plan in place can reduce anxiety because you have a ready blueprint to follow. This was a huge lesson in the parachute club –

every outcome or possibility was planned for. 'What's the worst that could happen, and how do we mitigate against it?'

- **Practice Mindfulness and Stress-Relief Techniques:**
  Techniques such as deep breathing, meditation, or even short walks can help in managing stress and maintaining a calm demeanour. I returned to the skies in my head – you don't need to do that but find something that works for you.

- **Stay Informed:**
  Keep yourself informed with accurate and up-to-date information about the crisis. Avoid information overload, but having the right information can reduce uncertainty, which is a significant source of stress.

- **Communicate Regularly:**
  Keep lines of communication open with your team. Regular updates can help in reducing rumours and misinformation, which can escalate anxiety. It is so crucial to only deal with the specific facts, and steer away from rumours, assumptions or other distractions.

- **Delegate Responsibilities:**
  Recognise that you cannot manage everything alone. Delegating effectively can help manage the workload and empower your team, which can alleviate stress.

- **Reflect on Past Experiences:**
  Draw on previous experiences of managing crises. Reflecting on what worked well and what didn't, can provide valuable insights and reinforce your confidence in handling the current situation.

- **Seek Support:**
  Don't hesitate to seek support from mentors or advisors who can offer guidance and reassurance. Sharing responsibilities and discussing concerns can help in maintaining a balanced perspective.

Staying calm as a leader doesn't mean suppressing emotions; it means understanding and managing them to ensure that your leadership remains effective and decisive during critical times.

As I mentioned earlier, I would often ask people this very effective question when they came to me with certain issues, 'Have you pulled your ripcord yet?' which meant had they slowed everything down so they could think clearly or were they still falling at 120 miles per hour. More often than not, they were still freefalling and needed help slowing down. Over the years I have managed to perfect this discipline and it has helped me navigate some particularly difficult situations.

If I can use an analogy to explain further, have you ever received an email that you took offence to? Of course you have, whether it be what was said in the email, or how it was said, but we have all been offended or upset by an email at some stage in our careers. And what's our response? We place this email at the top of our priority list, and we start to create an immediate response – how can that person speak to me like that? How dare they? I'll tell them!! And off we go. Email, as a form of communication, is not a method of immediate action. If you wanted a speedy response to an emergency, would you email somebody? No, you wouldn't, you would probably IM (Instant Message) or make a phone call. So why is it when there are so many unread or unanswered emails in our inbox that we feel the need to respond immediately to the one that has offended us? That's emotion for you. We all have it and that's what makes the world wonderful – we're all different but funnily enough, the majority of us react the same way when placed in certain scenarios.

Again, staying calm as a leader doesn't mean suppressing emotions; it means understanding and managing them to ensure that your leadership remains effective and decisive during critical times. The majority of cases brought by employees against their employers are based on leaders not being able to control their emotions, but going off the script and not following procedures, or saying or doing something stupid during a crisis. Don't be that person – every action does not require an immediate response, and there's always a holding pattern available to you to place the issue into before making the wrong decision or taking the wrong action. Always try to understand why you wanted to react with a certain emotion and get to the root cause. That will help you make an effective decision and give an appropriate response

Pull the ripcord and wait until you're floating through the skies with a clear head.

The rest of my first jump was uneventful, and I landed safely in the drop zone with the guidance from the instructor on the ground. As I continued my jumps, I did my second one with the instructor providing the directions for a safe landing, and on the third jump he believed that I could do it without the radio this time. Generally, a trainee would use the radio for the first 5 jumps, but I seemed to be getting the hang of it so he said, if you do your third jump without the need for any instruction from me, you can take the radio off in future. And so I did. Third jump and I descended on target into the drop zone landing safely and that was the end of the radio for me. It felt like a great sense of accomplishment, and although it was a small accomplishment, if felt so good. Perhaps it was the fact that both Sean and Kieran were still on the radio after their third jump, which helped too because it added bragging rights, especially as the 3 of us were being so competitive at this time.

Leadership Lesson – Recognise & Celebrate the Small Wins

It's so important when looking at a large task to accept and celebrate the small accomplishments along the way. Sometimes a task can be so big and the end line is so far away that it feels like there's no progress being made, and the work you're doing doesn't feel like it's recognised. Ever sat through a football game and the end result is nil-nil? Yeah – a couple of hours gone by that you'll never get back and nothing has been gained from it.

Recognising and celebrating small achievements is crucial for effective leadership, especially when learning to lead a team. Here are several reasons why this practice is so important:

- **Motivation and Engagement:**
  Celebrating small wins boosts the morale of team members. It helps them see that their efforts are noticed and appreciated, which in turn increases their motivation and engagement. A motivated team is more likely to be productive and committed to their work.

- **Positive Work Culture:**
  Regular recognition of achievements, even minor ones, fosters a positive work environment. It encourages an atmosphere of support and collaboration rather than competition. This can be especially important in high-stress environments where the risk of burnout is high.

- **Reinforcement of Desired Behaviours:**
  By celebrating small achievements, leaders can reinforce the behaviours and practices that led to those successes. This helps in establishing clear examples of what is valued within the team, guiding team members towards the behaviours that contribute to the team's goals.

- **Building Confidence:**
  Small achievements might seem trivial, but they can significantly boost the confidence of team members. Each success builds their confidence in their abilities and their belief in the team's capability to achieve future goals. This is particularly important for teams tackling large and complex projects.

- **Encouraging Innovation and Risk-Taking:**
  Recognising achievements can encourage team members to innovate and take risks. Knowing that their efforts are acknowledged, even if every initiative isn't a major success, team members may feel safer to experiment and think creatively.

- **Highlighting Progress:**
  In long-term projects it can be easy to lose sight of progress. Celebrating small milestones helps to visualise the advancement towards bigger goals, keeping the team focused and preventing discouragement.

- **Adaptability:**
  Celebrations provide an opportunity for leaders to reflect on what led to successes, however small. This can offer insights into team dynamics and processes that work, which can be adapted and applied to future challenges.

For leaders learning to manage teams, focusing on small achievements helps in building a supportive team dynamic and sets the foundation for achieving larger goals. It also provides valuable practice in observing and responding to the nuances of team management, essential for any leader's development.

So, as delighted as I was that I no longer needed a radio, on my next solo jump, my 4th in total, I had probably never needed the radio more, or so I had thought.

Again, at 3,000 feet, the instructor at that time was judging the spot. As usual she put her head out of the open door and guided the pilot to where she believed the appropriate spot was. I remember hearing a disagreement between her and the pilot, but she ultimately won. Again, I followed the same procedure, which I was getting used to at this stage, and exited the plane. Immediately I knew there was something wrong - I was downwind of the drop zone and being pushed back every second. Now, there's never any need to panic as the team at the parachute club are used to what is called 'bum spots,' and if you get lost, it's not long until your found. However, the surrounding fields are all marshlands and bogs, so they weren't the best areas to be landing.

So here I was, parachute open and heading backwards in the wrong direction when thankfully the training kicked in. If I had any chance of making it back even close to the drop zone, I needed to fight against the wind and use a technique called 'crabbing'. A canopy is crabbing when it is flown at an angle sideways to the ambient wind, resulting in a path across the ground that is sideways as well as forwards, just like a crab walks. So, as I was attempting to 'crab', for the first time, every time I positioned directly into the wind I was pushed backed further. I persevered and kept trying and soon it was working, and I was making slow but gradual progress back to where I needed to be. I was cursing the instructor 'from a height', I assume that's where that expression came from, and fighting against the natural direction that the wind wanted to send me. And it was hard work and certainly not what I had expected. Without any guidance from the ground, and first time off the radio, I needed to remember my training and work the rest out for myself.

As I got closer and closer to the drop zone, so too did my altitude and as I battled to get across the road and into the safety of the drop zone I realised that I was too low and right below my feet were electricity power lines. I was at about 200 feet and moving nowhere – the wind was now blowing directly into my face at approximately 20mph, and the parachute would normally move forward at 20mph, so therefore I was stranded above electricity power lines below my feet, descending and neither going forward or backwards.

Assessing risk is a crucial part of leadership and sometimes if can be difficult to truly identify the risks ahead of you, but in this situation, it was a lot easier.

I had two options: stay where I was and slowly lower myself onto the power lines or find somewhere else to land. I looked around and saw a field behind me which had a few cows in it, so I grabbed one of the toggles, pulled it down sharply, and while I expected a nice smooth circular turn in the sky, the wind instantly took a hold of me, and I moved from 0mph to 40mph. As the wind was pushing me past the field, I needed to pull down hard again on the same toggle to place myself back into the wind so that I could land safely. Within a matter of seconds I had propelled across the entire field and was now at the back of this field, but coming in to land safely. I had flown straight over the heads of these cows and to be honest I have never seen cows' heads move in the way that they did that day, and I don't think I ever will again.

I laugh to myself even to this day when I think of one cow saying to another, 'Wow, look at him moooove' (sorry, couldn't resist it). I came in to land and landed very softly, probably due to the strength of the wind and not my skydiving prowess, and it was time for the walk back to the drop zone. As I gathered my parachute into my hands, I noticed that these cows were all running over to me; I also noticed that these black and white cows all had horns on their heads. I didn't think that bulls were black and white, and the reason I landed there, not that I'd had much choice, was they looked like harmless cows. I then looked to my parachute and instantly realised it was coloured red. I tried to disguise the colouring of the parachute, but it was too big, so I made a run for it. I was running across the field holding a red parachute being chasing by about a dozen bulls, almost like an obscure Irish bull fight or some crazy comedy routine, where the Irish matador was so scared of bull fighting that he ran for his life every time he entered the arena.

Occasionally I would stop and turn to see if they were still chasing me, and they'd all stop. Every time I ran, they ran after me. I tried to 'Ssshhhush' them and waved my hands, but I dropped the parachute and had to pick it back up again. As I looked down and took my eyes off them, they moved closer. So, I struggled to pick up the parachute with my hands whilst looking directly at them and I tripped over it when I tried to run again. I could swear one of them was laughing at me. I reckon if they thought that I had just arrived down from the skies and I was an alien invading the country, they would definitely fancy their chances against me. Perhaps we've already been invaded in the past, and the bulls had our backs, fought them off and we never ever heard about it. This went on for a few more minutes and then finally I reached the gate and thankfully none of them managed to get too close to me to cause any injury.

I walked into the drop zone, which was just across the road, and below those power lines I had managed to avoid and told the club members of what I'd just gone through. Never mind the dangers of a 'bum spot' but the added drama of being chased out of the field by a dozen bulls. 'Bulls?' they said, 'what bulls? There are no bulls around here' and I told them about the dozen I had just encountered. 'What colour were they, ya feckin' Dublin eejit?' I said they were black and white, and they fell around laughing at me. 'They're cows, ya feckin' eejit – typical Dub, wouldn't know a cow from a budgie – they're nosy animals and just wanted to see what you were doing and that's why they were following you. Cows have horns too, but they're usually cut off. If it was a bull, he'd have worn you like a horn sock'.

I've never been so embarrassed – here was me just surviving a traumatic experience of firstly battling myself back to the drop zone, and doing well to do so in my opinion, then fighting off a bunch of angry bulls, which didn't exist, all just after jumping out of a plane – jaysus, I needed a drink. As much as I tried to forget that experience, I was reminded quite regularly about it. And sure, if I was them, I'd certainly have kept bringing it up too. As stupid as it was, it was also quite funny.

They told me afterwards that it wouldn't have mattered whether I had the radio or not as I had done everything that they would have told me to do anyway.

It taught me a lot though, and other than actually knowing what a cow is now, I learnt to 'crab' the canopy, and although it wasn't an enjoyable canopy ride down, and in all honesty, it felt as though my usually enjoyable canopy ride had been taken away from me because of the bad spot, these things happen and you have to learn to accept that people are human, and mistakes can be made. I was safe... and that's all that matters.

My next jump which was my final standard static line jump went very smoothly and I progressed to the 'Dummy Ripcord Pull (DRP) stage successfully. This stage of jumps as mentioned before were for the instructors to see that I could reach the ripcord and pull it whilst still having the safety of the static line to open my parachute. Again, it was five in a row before progressing to freefall so I needed to maintain concentration. I really wanted to get to the freefall stage for a couple of reasons – one, this would be the first real step to achieving my goal of replicating the tandem jump on my own, albeit being from a lower altitude, but it was the first step of freefall; and second, both Sean and Kieran were progressing well too, and although we all said that we'd love to do our first together, we all still wanted to be the first and screw the other two.

My job at the time meant that I needed to work some weekends, so I wasn't able to be at the club every weekend, whilst the other two were. They were slightly hampered by the weather, so they hadn't gotten too far ahead of me, but the pressure was on. However I knew that I needed to ensure that the pressure didn't affect my judgement and decision making. I was eager to be the first and I'd some hurdles to jump in relation to availability and getting to the club each weekend, but I knew I couldn't risk making mistakes that would impact my progression. If I made a mistake during these 5 jumps I would have to start from the beginning again and I surely wouldn't keep up with the other 2 then.

And here's the funny thing, and only in hindsight did I realise this... that was my reason for not making mistakes! Let me remind you... my reason for not making mistakes was so that I would stay within touch of the other 2 and not lose my opportunity of being the first to freefall. Let's just think about that for a moment.

It wasn't that I might make a mistake and die... it was so I would not lose my competitive edge, the opportunity of being the first to freefall. Unintentionally I had allowed other minor goals to distract me from the ultimate objective, which was staying alive long enough to achieve my main objective. Seriously, who cares who was first? It ended up that it was Kieran who did his a few weeks before Sean and I. But in the long run it didn't matter. For us it was a massive milestone, but for everyone else in the club it was like taking the stabilisers off a bike – you're not even close to riding the bike yet.

Leadership Lesson – Distractions

Staying focused on ultimate goals and avoiding distractions from minor issues is a fundamental aspect of effective leadership. Here's why it's important and the potential dangers of losing focus:

- **Preserving Resources:**
  Leadership involves managing limited resources, including time, money, and human effort. Minor distractions can lead to wasteful expenditure of these resources, which might otherwise be invested in achieving more significant, strategic goals.

- **Maintaining Momentum:**
  Achieving big goals often requires building and maintaining momentum. Getting sidetracked by minor issues can disrupt this momentum, making it harder to achieve the main objectives. This can lead to delays and decreased morale among team members.

- **Clarity and Direction:**
  Effective leaders provide a clear vision and direction for their team or organisation. If a leader is frequently distracted by lesser issues, it can create confusion and inconsistency, undermining the team's trust and commitment.

- **Opportunity Costs:**
  When leaders focus on trivial matters, they miss out on potentially crucial opportunities that could be more beneficial to their goals. The opportunity cost of being bogged down by minor details can be substantial, potentially causing the organisation to fall behind its competitors.

- **Risk of Poor Decision Making:**
  Leaders who cannot prioritise may end up making decisions based on what's immediately in front of them rather than what's most important. This can lead to poor strategic choices that jeopardize long-term success.

- **Setting a Precedent:**
  A leader's approach to handling issues sets a precedent for the rest of the organisation. If a leader pays excessive attention to minor problems, it can encourage a similar focus among team members, diverting the entire organisation's attention away from its primary goals.

The dangers of veering off track include the risk of failing to achieve key objectives, diluting the organisation's efforts, and potentially leading the organisation into crises that could have been avoided with a more disciplined, focused approach. Thus, a leader's ability to discern between what requires immediate attention and what can be delegated or ignored is crucial for effective leadership and organisational success.

Allow me to digress a little away from skydiving, but remain on the topic of distraction, albeit coming from a different source.

Leadership Lesson – Intentional Distraction Training

I recently spoke to a friend of mine who was a member of London's Metropolitan Police firearms unit, the Specialist Firearms Command. The Specialist Firearms Command are an elite cadre of highly trained police officers on standby to respond to any armed incident in London.

It was during one of these training courses that my friend told me the following story, and I thought that it demonstrates the power of deliberate distraction and how easy it can be to fall foul of when under pressure. In an age when technology is pulling us from one solution to another and from one gadget to another, it's so important not to forget the fundamentals.

He explained the recruitment process and how only the best were accepted onto courses after a rigorous application, including a legislation exam, an interview, and a tabletop exercise. Despite the firearms department requiring 30 new officers, if 50 applied and only 20 got through that part, they would only take 20. There was no 'dumbing down' to achieve numbers – they required only the very best. Those going forward into weapons handling, shooting, and tactics had been selected on the basis that they were all capable and could be turned into firearms officers. The course was structured in such a way to add pressure every day, to elicit the best from the trainees, and make them think before acting, down to split second level.

Life or death scenarios!

After a few weeks of learning the weapons, mastering the shooting, tactical reloads and many more skills development, the course moved onto the search element employing the theory and all the previously developed skills.

This one class of 6 officers, male and female, with years of policing experience without firearms under their belts were to search a single storey multi room building for a suspect, believed to be armed. As they underwent the briefing, an instructor entered the room carrying a box and announced that the new torches had arrived, and this bunch could try them out. Attaching the torches to the underside of their Glock pistols and being shown how to activate them with one finger, the briefing concluded and off they went.

On a gloomy, wet, dark afternoon in the middle of November, the officers lined up and entered the building. Torches on, they meticulously searched the building for an hour and, satisfied that they had cleared it and no suspect had been discovered, they returned to the briefing room for their debrief. The expletives flowed from the instructors immediately.

What could possibly have gone wrong?

It took them twice as long to clear the building as the course required. Despite there never being a suspect in the building all along, they took an hour to clear a building which they should have cleared in half the time. The group felt that they had cleared the room as efficiently as they could, given the fact that it was a dark afternoon in November, and they only had torchlight to see.

The instructors felt differently about the group's opinions.

These highly trained police officers had all been distracted by a new toy. Not one of them attempted to turn on the building lights as they moved through the rooms. If they had done so, they would have cleared the building in the acceptable time.

The power of distraction is immense. Not one of them had stepped back for a moment, considered that if they hadn't been provided with torches, they would have turned the building lights on. Every single one of them was required to be a leader in that exercise and not one showed the level of leadership required. The lesson ended and what was taken away from it was: think about the basics first; just because you have all the tools and bells and whistles, you don't always need them.

Six people, one leader, 5 followers and no one thought to question it. They followed blindly, trusting the front player as each took a turn as team leader. Bad decision making at leadership level is easily avoidable. We need to have leaders who can create the next leader, not lead them blindly.

This was a regular test conducted by the instructors for this very purpose... to identify true leaders. It's fine during a training exercise but imagine if the life of a hostage was at stake and the rescuers were easy to distract. It's the same for leaders in all organisations. Luckily, most of you will never experience the pressure of making decisions that could be the difference between life and death.

The impact of leaders getting distracted cannot be overstated. It jeopardises strategic focus, undermines team morale, and compromises decision-making. However by adopting strategies to mitigate these distractions, leaders can safeguard their attention, enhance their effectiveness, and drive their organisations toward success.

In doing so they not only set a powerful example for their teams but also create a competitive advantage in today's fast-paced business landscape. As we navigate through the noise the ability to remain focused and present will distinguish the good leaders from the truly great ones.

I was distracted however I maintained a professional and cautious approach to this distraction and ensured, albeit for possibly the wrong reason, that I did every jump as carefully and as correctly as I could. It never ever registered with me that by doing this I was also keeping myself alive... I just wanted to keep up with the others.

And that's what happened. I kept up with the others and finally did my freefall on the same day as Sean, totally oblivious of the method of progression Sean had taken. But that's his story, and that story is coming soon.

I didn't have any real excitement during these jumps, other than the obvious. I didn't crack my elbow off a sheep's head, I didn't slip off the strut, I didn't land face down in shit, I didn't perform a downwind landing and almost castrate myself on a barbed wire fence (sorry, I didn't mention that the fence was barbed wire beforehand whilst telling Jack's story), but I did have a lot of fun and I did float straight through a beautiful, fluffy white cloud which I will never forget. I'll do my utmost best to describe this feeling as I recognise that there are very few people in the world who will get to experience this for themselves. Most people's experience comes from sitting inside a plane, feeling the little bit of turbulence and sometimes thinking, I wonder if I could just sit on that. Firstly, the answer to that question is a most definite no.

Floating through a fluffy white cloud while in a parachute is the most exhilarating and surreal experience. As you descend gently through the cloud, the world around seems to just fade away, enveloping you in a soft, dense fog. The visibility diminishes, leaving you with a sense of isolation and tranquillity that's akin to being in a quiet, ethereal world apart from the earth below.

The air inside the cloud is cool and moist, with tiny droplets of water misting your face and skin, refreshing, like a spiritual cleansing, contrasting with the rush of adrenaline from the parachute descent. The sounds may become muffled while inside the cloud, enhancing the sense of serenity and detachment from the usual noises of the world.

Emerging from the cloud, the sudden clarity and expansiveness of the view can be breathtaking. The brightness of the sun and the vivid colours of the landscape below return sharply into focus, offering a striking contrast to the soft, monochrome world inside the cloud.

This moment of transition can heighten the sense of awe and appreciation for the vast beauty of the sky and the earth — an unforgettable blend of peace, thrill, and wonder.

I will truly never forget this moment, and although it felt like it lasted for hours, it was only a few seconds, and I then needed to find my bearings again, figure out where I was and find the drop zone once more.

Although this was a moment that I would never forget, I had inadvertently breached some of the club's rules, although in fairness to me, I hadn't yet been taught them. There are rules for flying through cloud (yes, it even feels strange writing those words), but this is a place where they have such rules, and these rules are nor negotiable.

The rule for flying a canopy through a thick cloud, which is taught once you start jumping with others, is:

1. start making a gentle right turn
2. scream or sing

Screaming would be an equivalent of a foghorn on a boat and allows everyone to know that you're there. If you know the cloud is thin, you can proceed straight on.

After successfully completing my 5 DRP jumps, it was now time for the big one... the first freefall. And that's a whole new kettle of fish. The nerves and apprehension in preparation for this jump is beyond description. Luckily for me, I had recently had my 'smell the farts' conversation with an instructor, and my mind was focussed on the task ahead.

It took a few weeks before I was able to get back to the club due to a run of weekend work which I couldn't avoid. All that was on my mind for these weeks was this upcoming jump. I'll have to be honest with you that the more time that went by, the easier it was to not do it. As I had broken the momentum my mind was providing me with perfectly acceptable reasons not to return to the club – they'll have forgotten about me... sure, most of the guys have already given up and you've done more than them, so that's ok... you've already proven that you can do it... why risk it? It was easy just not to return, and funnily enough, because we had somewhat distanced ourselves from the majority of the members of the club, nobody was really calling me up about it or pushing me, and maybe that's what I needed. Sometimes breaking momentum can go against you and I think that my mind was taking the opportunity, and probably rightly so, to use this break in momentum to speak some sense to me. It never had the chance before because I was fully immersed in the club, but now it was like an itch that wouldn't go away. The longer I stayed away from the club, the itch became more irritating, and my confidence began to wane.

Leadership Lesson – Maintaining Momentum

Maintaining momentum in leadership is also so important when trying to achieve a goal for several reasons:

- **Consistency and Progress:**
  Momentum helps to ensure that progress towards the goal is consistent. When a team maintains momentum, it can build upon previous successes, making each step forward more impactful.

- **Motivation:**
  Momentum can significantly boost the morale of a team. Seeing tangible progress and achievements can motivate team members to continue working hard and commit to the goal. It helps to keep energy levels high and can prevent burnout.

- **Overcoming Obstacles:**
  With strong momentum teams are better equipped to handle setbacks and challenges. The drive and pace can help them to quickly recover and adapt, turning potential failures into learning opportunities.

- **Building Confidence:**
  Steady momentum can help build confidence within the team. As members see that their efforts are leading to success, their confidence in their abilities and in the leadership increases. I could feel my confidence slipping as time passed by.

- **Attracting Support:**
  In many scenarios maintaining momentum can also help in garnering support from stakeholders and upper management. Success tends to attract more attention and resources, which can be critical in achieving the goal.

- **Time Efficiency:**
  Momentum helps to minimise delays and maximises the efficient use of time. It encourages prompt decision-making and action, which can be vital in time-sensitive projects.

Leadership plays a key role in building and sustaining this momentum by setting clear goals, providing resources, motivating the team, and leading by example. Effective leaders also adapt strategies as needed to ensure the momentum is not lost, even in the face of difficulties.

There were only two options, give it up or get my ass back down to the club. Kieran had already done his first freefall, and I missed his initiation ceremony. Sean was struggling a little and still hadn't done his. The pusher for me was when Sean completed his DRP jumps and he told me that next was his first freefall – that revelation ignited my fire again, which I desperately needed, and I said, 'right, see you at the weekend'.

I retrieved the bottle of Irish Cream Poitin which I had previously bought in preparation of this day, wrapped it in masking tape, ensured I was off work at the weekend, and the remaining 3 of us left early on Saturday morning for the drop zone. Halfway down the road to the club, I remember thinking whether this bottle had a 'best before' date as there certainly wasn't one printed on the bottle. Laughing to myself, I thought, well, if the jump doesn't kill me, maybe the concoction in this bottle might.

Walking to the manifest office and saying, '3 freefalls please', actually felt quite special. They already knew the level we were at, and thinking back, they probably thought that it was a stupid thing to say, but we didn't care – it meant so much for us. It was a thing we had spoken about for a long time and now here we were, all 3 of us, getting into a plane together to jump out, static line free, into the world of freefall. We had successfully passed our 'probation', for want of a better word, and this jump made us legitimate skydivers... all we had to do was survive. And not just the jump, but the initiation later that night in the pub. The weather was perfect and within about 2 hours we were ready to go.

Kieran had done a few at this stage, so he was jumping from a higher altitude than myself and Sean as we were on the first, a 3 second freefall. As previously mentioned, this was a similar timing to the static line jumps, with the same count – one one thousand, two one thousand, three one thousand, but the difference was, we needed to get the ripcord as there was no static line to do it for us.

Getting into the plane was a little different. There was no static line attached to my back, and no lines from other people to navigate around once in the plane. Kieran got in first, as he would be last out because he would climb to a higher altitude after myself and Sean jumped out at 3,000 feet; Sean got in second, which meant he would jump out second, and I got in last, which meant I was going first.

The attitude was different too. The instructor and pilot really seemed to treat us differently, and this may have been in my mind, but it did feel that way. There was very little instructional talk and all the instructor really said about the jump was, 'now remember lads, get the ripcord – that's it, and if you miss it more than once, go for the reserve – no messing about now – the rest you know what to do at this stage – well done for getting to this point – you'll be great'. It was actually a nice little motivational speech, and although it may not seem like it, to myself and Sean, it was all we needed. Kieran, on the other hand, who had already done a few freefalls was less motivational. 'Don't catch your balls in the straps lads', he added whilst nearly convulsing in laughter. Kieran was a really straight-laced kind of guy, and he didn't come up with the wise cracks as much as others, but when he did, they were usually very funny – this one wasn't that funny, but anytime Kieran cracked a gag, he was usually the one who laughed hardest. I think he was still giggling to himself when I jumped about 5 or 6 minutes later. That made me smile – not the wise crack but the fact he found it so funny. You'd love Kieran if you ever met him, and when it came to skydiving, he was a machine, and nothing got in his way – I'll tell you his story shortly.

Out I climbed onto the strut, same as I had done before, and when I looked inside the plane, the instructor just smiled and said, 'Feck Off', and off I fecked – the pleasantries were gone and were not a part of the team. I let go - one one thousand, two one thousand, three one thousand, I pulled my right hand down to my side to grab the ripcord whilst raising my up left hand up across my head to maintain my aerodynamic position, found the cord, pulled the life out of it, and the parachute opened successfully – no problems. For the rest of the canopy ride down I had such a feeling of accomplishment, and I whipped that parachute around the sky swinging from side to side, doing numerous spirals and having the time of my life.

The adrenaline stayed with me all day and into the night. The initiation ceremony was a fantastic night, and although I didn't get the chance to jump again that day, prior to entering the pub, I fully intended to get another freefall in the following day to top off the weekend. Unfortunately, that didn't happen, and it wasn't Mother Nature that prevented it, it was Daddy Drink who gave me such a killer of a hangover that all I could do was stay in bed.

While we were in the pub, Sean and I discussed every detail of the jump – we talked about the training and how important that training was and how thankful we were that we'd done it, knowing that if it wasn't for that training, we would never have felt so comfortable to do the jump. Knowing we had successfully completed each of our DRP jumps gave us the confidence to know that when they took the static line away, it wasn't going to be an issue. Yeah, brave talk *after* we had done it, but beforehand it was a very different feeling.

In hindsight, when I look back to that discussion, I remember that it was really just me talking and Sean just listening. If I had taken the time to realise that I may have asked him why he wasn't as excited and as confident as me, but I didn't as I was too wrapped up in my own accomplishments and I wasn't really listening to Sean, or perhaps not really hearing what he was trying to tell me. Only in hindsight did I look back and think to myself – I think he was trying to tell me something that night, but I never gave him the chance.

Leadership Lesson – Don't Get So Wrapped Up In Yourself

When leaders become excessively focused on their own accomplishments to the point where they fail to listen to the concerns of others, several specific risks and negative impacts can arise, affecting both the leader's effectiveness and the overall health of the organisation:

- **Communication Breakdown:**
  Effective leadership relies heavily on open lines of communication. When leaders do not listen to others, it can lead to a breakdown in communication within the organisation. Important information might not be relayed, leading to uninformed decisions that could negatively impact the organisation.

- **Decreased Employee Morale and Engagement:**
  Employees who feel that their voices are unheard or that their concerns are consistently disregarded may become disengaged and demotivated. This lack of engagement can result in reduced productivity, higher turnover rates, and a decline in overall workplace morale.

- **Blind Spots in Leadership:**
  Leaders who ignore other perspectives often develop blind spots. They may fail to recognise emerging challenges or problems because they are not receiving full feedback from their team. This can delay necessary changes and prevent the leader from effectively addressing issues that could have been mitigated early on.

- **Innovation Stifling:**
  Innovation thrives in environments where ideas are freely exchanged, and diverse perspectives are welcomed. A leader who does not listen to others is likely missing out on innovative ideas and creative solutions

that could be beneficial to the organisation. This stifles growth and adaptability and frustrates team members, who are not encouraged to present or develop their ideas.

- **Toxic Work Environment:**
  When a leader dismisses or ignores the concerns of others it can foster a toxic work environment. Such environments are characterized by mistrust, frustration, and a lack of respect, which can further erode team cohesion and effectiveness, and lead to high employee turnover, thus costing the company in time and money.

- **Risk of Groupthink:**
  A leader who doesn't listen to others might unintentionally encourage a culture of groupthink, where conformity is valued over critical analysis and dissent. This can lead to poor decision-making and a lack of creativity, as team members may feel pressured to agree with the leader rather than offer genuine insights or raise valid concerns. Sean was conforming to the culture that I was driving at this time.

- **Loss of Trust and Credibility:**
  Leaders who fail to address or even acknowledge the concerns of their teams risk losing trust and credibility. Once trust is eroded it can be very difficult to rebuild, affecting the leader's ability to effectively manage and inspire their team.

These issues highlight the importance of empathetic and responsive leadership, which includes actively listening to team members and stakeholders, acknowledging their concerns, and incorporating their feedback into decision-making processes. Such practices not only enhance the leader's effectiveness but also contribute to a healthier, more dynamic organisational culture.

Sean had something to tell me but I never allowed him the opportunity, and perhaps if I had, it would have changed the future. Sean stayed away for a couple of weeks and only after his next jump did I find out why.

The following weekend I went back down to the club and did my 5 second freefall. I made a bit of a mess of it, possibly because my overconfidence made me a little cocky and complacent, so they failed me on that jump, and I had to repeat it. I had exited the plane incorrectly, something I'd done so many times before, I pulled the cord too quickly by not maintaining composure and sticking to the count, I just did everything too fast. I don't know why, but I did. I never got the chance to try it again that weekend because of the weather, but I did the following weekend and I progressed to the next level which was an 8 second freefall.

It was another couple of weekends until I got back to the club to do this jump, and after a bit of pushing Sean came down with me – my thoughts at that time were Sean was probably going through what I had experienced, and because he had broken his momentum he was becoming a bit hesitant, so I thought it was best to get him 'back up on the horse', as the expression goes. Again, I was blind to anything else at this time, but also, how could I have known what was truly going on in Sean's head. I wasn't allowing him to tell me. I was placing pressure on him, and in hindsight that was the last thing he needed.

> I will never forget that jump and it will go to the grave with me. Kieran, Sean and I went up in the plane together and because Sean was doing a 5 second freefall, he jumped first, and Kieran and I sat in the plane helpless as we watched the events unfold. We both jumped afterwards and raced down through the skies to Sean who was lying motionless on the ground below us as people ran from the hangers out to where he had landed.

Sean's story is coming up, but as I mentioned, I will never ever forget that day and it's possibly a large part of the reason of why I'm writing this book. I continued my progressions, because I was determined. However another experience was occurring as my jump heights got higher. When initially jumping from a plane for a 3 second freefall by the time your parachute opens, you are still very much vertical as you've just been hanging from the strut of the plane. The longer your freefall time, the more time you have for your body to become horizontal, and that's another amazing feeling. I was probably on my 12 second freefall before I could look out across the sky and see the horizon, which meant I was totally horizontal; it was another breathtaking moment – one which I'll also never forget, however, each time I jumped after the incident with Sean I just couldn't get the fear out of me. Every time I got into the plane after that day, it was like the very first time again. It was getting so bad that I was forgetting what the farts smelt like, never mind realising that they were there at all. All of my built-up confidence was gone and I was starting from scratch again, except I didn't have the safety of the static line. I should have spoken up at the time, but I was genuinely afraid to – I didn't think that anyone would understand how I was feeling, so I tried to keep pushing through myself. I knew I was putting myself at risk and I had forgotten about my initial goal of replicating the tandem as a solo jump – I just wanted to get each jump out of the way as I progressed so that the fear would leave me again, as it had done so in the past.

I had to re-do my 12 second freefall, because again I made a mess of it. Yes, it was a great experience seeing the horizon again, but I wasn't concentrating – I was thinking about Sean and not thinking about the task at hand. I progressed to the 15 second freefall and completed that with an even longer and even more beautiful view of the horizon. Unfortunately, I failed that jump too because I was too late pulling the cord and didn't do so until 20 seconds. Obviously, that was a fail, but the instructors laughed it off saying, 'Wow, didn't think you were going to pull it at all... don't be too confident and remember your count'. I wasn't confident... I was the opposite... I was terrified, but the horizon distracted me and I wanted to stay there forever. I just stopped counting as I looked across the skies and really just forgot where I was. I remember thinking, 'Oops, nearly forgot something', and immediately reached down to pull the cord. I knew I'd messed it up when the parachute opened as I checked my altitude and I was about 900 feet lower than I should have been at this time. I redid the 15 second freefall again and successfully passed this time.

The next jump was for my qualification, which was a 20 second 'unstable' freefall. I joked that I had already done a 20 second, but the response was, 'Maybe, but not on purpose and it wasn't unstable'. This jump was the final 'trainee' jump and a requirement if you wanted to be a qualified sky-diver, which I really wanted to be. I still hadn't reached the height of 10,000 feet on my own yet, and once I'd completed this jump, I would have been able to go up in the next plane up to that height. I would have achieved my goal. This jump no longer required you to hang off the strut of the plane – this jump required you to stand at the edge of the door, put one hand on your helmet and the other hand across your body and grab your ankle. Once in this position, the instructor would push you out of the plane and you would tumble out into the sky in an unstable fashion. The reason for this was to ensure that you could stabilise yourself whilst in freefall, which was actually quite simple – all you need to do was arch, and that was it.

Kieran had done his weeks and weeks ago and he always spoke about how amazing it was. Kieran was already up to 10,000 feet and having a ball – his story is next up.

My work again got in the way of my trips down to the club and again momentum was broken, but this time there was more to it. I already had doubts and now the lack of momentum was helping my mind make more sense when it was convincing me to quit. Also the added thoughts in my head about what happened to Sean and the fact that it was only Kieran still left in the club, and he was so focussed and was progressing so well, I found the excuses easier and easier to find each weekend and that was that. Every experience except one was absolutely amazing and I thoroughly enjoyed my journey, but after 36 solo jumps and 2 tandem jumps, and reaching a height of 7,000 feet for my 15 second freefall, and with only one more hurdle to go, I gave into my fears and the pressure my mind was putting on me, and I never returned to the club again.

I failed in my goal, and it was purely down to me. I can blame others if I want to make it easier on myself, but no good will come from that. Yes, I was affected by external actions and events, but those are only excuses and not reasons. If I was to be true to myself, I used those excuses to convince myself to quit, for one main reason – I was scared and I couldn't shake it. Perhaps prior to the incident with Sean my confidence was more bravado than confidence. Perhaps the fear had never left me – it felt like it had – but perhaps it hadn't and perhaps all I needed was the thoughts of what happened to Sean possibly happening to me to reintroduce me to my true feeling, but I suppose I'll never know. I'll always remember the experience and the lessons that time has taught me, however, I don't think I will ever jump again. That last time was 23 years ago now and I will never ever forget it – all in all it was absolutely amazing.

Fear can get to all of us, and in leadership it's so important to do your best to overcome it. Although I gave into fear while skydiving, I have never let it get the better of me since, and if I was to think about the greatest lesson this experience has taught me, well then, it's that.

Leadership Lesson – Control Your Fear

Leaders can sometimes fail due to their personal fears and hesitations, particularly when these fears prevent them from pursuing goals or taking actions, they genuinely desire. There is nothing wrong with fear, in fact it's quite healthy, but you need to have control over it.

This failure can manifest in several ways:

- **Loss of Opportunity:**
  Fear can cause leaders to avoid taking risks or seizing opportunities that could lead to significant advancements for their organisation or their career. This avoidance can result in stagnation and missed chances for growth.

- **Undermining Authority:**
  When leaders are visibly fearful or indecisive it can erode their authority and credibility. Team members may begin to doubt the leader's capabilities, which can undermine team morale and effectiveness.

- **Poor Decision Making:**
  Fear can skew a leader's judgment, leading to overly cautious or suboptimal decision-making. This may also involve avoiding tough decisions altogether which can be detrimental to progress and innovation.

- **Stress and Burnout:**
  Continuous fear and hesitation can lead to high levels of personal stress and eventually burnout, which can impair a leader's ability to function effectively.

Solutions to Overcome Fear in Leadership

To overcome these challenges, leaders can adopt several strategies:

- **Self-Awareness:**
  Recognising one's fears is the first step towards managing them. Leaders can benefit from reflecting on what scares them and understanding how these fears impact their decisions and leadership style.

- **Seeking Feedback and Mentorship:**
  Engaging with mentors, peers or coaches can provide leaders with perspective and advice on how to handle their fears. Feedback can also help leaders recognise when their fears are influencing their decisions more than they should.

- **Building Confidence through Small Wins:**
  Leaders can gradually take on challenges that are slightly out of their comfort zone. Successfully navigating these smaller challenges can build confidence and reduce the impact of fear on bigger decisions.

- **Mindfulness and Stress Management Techniques:**
  Practices such as mindfulness, meditation, and regular physical activity can help leaders manage stress and anxiety, making them less likely to be overwhelmed by fear.

- **Decision-Making Frameworks:**
  Adopting structured approaches to decision-making can help leaders assess risks and benefits more objectively, reducing the likelihood of fear skewing their judgments.

- **Fostering a Supportive Culture:**
  Creating an organisational culture that supports risk-taking and acknowledges that failure is part of learning can help leaders feel safer to act despite their fears.

- **Professional Development in Emotional Intelligence:** Enhancing emotional intelligence can help leaders manage not only their fears but also understand and alleviate the fears of others, promoting a more courageous and proactive workplace.

Leadership is as much about managing one's own fears and doubts as it is about guiding others. By actively addressing the personal aspects of leadership, leaders can ensure that their fears do not hold them back from achieving their full potential.

If all you learn from this book is how to manage your fear of leadership, and potentially your fear of failure, then I'm delighted that I was able to help.

Now, for the final few chapters, let's explore Kieran's, and Sean's, experiences.

CHAPTER 12

THE MACHINE

From the very beginning, Kieran was a machine. And I don't just mean in his skydiving career, but generally in life. When Kieran gets something into his head, there's no stopping him, and once he's committed, he's all the way in.

Kieran completed about 180 jumps and became a fully qualified and extremely adept skydiver, exactly what I wish I had done. Throughout his journey he completed his tasks without any issues, was the first and only one of us to learn how to pack a parachute; the rest of us were either too lazy, thought it was too complicated or hadn't actually been pushed by the club at this stage to learn. To be honest, we were all just too lazy. When the weather was too bad to jump, we were all sitting drinking tea or coffee, watching reruns of old Gaelic football games on the TV and talking nonsense, while Kieran was in the hanger learning how to pack. In hindsight Kieran really loved every aspect of skydiving, whereas I think the rest of us just really loved the idea of being a skydiver; there's a big difference. And he got to be very good at it as I'm sure the rest of us would have been too if we'd bothered our backsides to do it.

By doing this Kieran had inadvertently broken away from our little clique and was mingling with the other members of the club and learning more about skydiving than just packing chutes. Unconsciously, he was learning about the life of a skydiver, the different types of chutes out there, the capability of each of them, the inner workings of a chute, and how to optimise it's use. He even at times joined the other skydivers when they were doing practice formations on the hanger floor using wooden dollies, if they needed an extra person in case a member of the formation team wasn't at the club that day. This team would lie on these dollies and spin themselves around the hanger floor simulating what they were planning to do in the skies. Kieran loved this, and in fairness to him, he loved everything else about the club.

I remember there were days after the incident with Sean, and the rest of our friends had quit, that Kieran and I would travel to the club and I wouldn't see him from one end of the day until the next as he was out doing things with his 'new' friends, which I really should have been doing myself but never bothered. Perhaps if I had, I'd have been more enthused to continue my journey; perhaps I was waiting for someone to come to me to push me to do so, but I had left myself outside of the loop other than a few people who genuinely had no real interest in whether or not I was jumping; they just enjoyed the craic we were having. They were already fully qualified, so they weren't too interested in my progression – they just saw someone who would enjoy a few drinks with them, talk nonsense (I was always very good at that) and shoot the breeze.

Although this may sound like a 'poor me' story, it most definitely is not – I had such fun at the time, but my fun was facing the totally opposite direction to the reason I was there. I think that if I had made more of an effort to hang onto Kieran's coat tails and follow his lead, I would have achieved my goals, however, I picked the wrong side. That was my decision, and that's a decision I need to own.

Leadership Lesson – Picking Your Side

This can happen a lot in leadership when new, but not always new, leaders associate themselves within a group of other leaders, who they may or may not look up to and who influence them in a direction which contradicts their own.

When this happens several issues can arise.

- **Loss of Vision and Focus:**
  New leaders usually start with a clear vision or set of goals for their organisation. Influential, qualified leaders can inadvertently or purposefully sway them away from these goals. This could lead to a diluted vision that no longer reflects the initial aims of the new leader, potentially leading to strategic misalignments.

- **Reduced Credibility and Authority:**
  If it becomes apparent that the new leader is frequently swayed by others their credibility can suffer. Stakeholders may begin to see them as lacking conviction or the ability to stand their ground, which can undermine their authority and leadership effectiveness.

- **Internal Conflict:**
  A leader who is pulled in directions contrary to their original goals may create internal conflict within the organisation. This could manifest as confusion among team members about the organisation's direction, disagreements within the leadership team, and a general lack of cohesion.

- **Erosion of Trust:**
  Trust within the organisation can erode if stakeholders feel that the leader is not consistent or is too easily influenced by others. This lack of trust can extend to doubts about the leader's capability to make autonomous decisions that are in the best interest of the organisation.

- **Decision-Making Paralysis:**
  A new leader who receives conflicting advice from more qualified leaders might find themselves unable to make decisions swiftly or effectively. This indecisiveness can stall important initiatives and slow down organisational momentum.

- **Stress and Job Dissatisfaction:**
  Leaders caught between their original goals and the influence of others might experience increased stress and dissatisfaction with their role. This personal struggle can detract from their job performance and overall well-being.

- **Loss of Unique Leadership Identity:**
  Every leader brings a unique set of strengths and perspectives to their role. Being overly influenced by others can lead to a loss of these unique qualities, making the leader less effective and possibly leading to a leadership style that is not authentic or effective for their specific context.

For new leaders it's crucial to balance the insights and advice from more experienced leaders with their own understanding and goals. Developing a robust advisory system, having a clear strategic vision, and continually reflecting on their core objectives can help new leaders maintain their course and effectively utilise the expertise of more experienced leaders without being led astray.

It's also so crucial to remember that this is your race to run, and only you can run it. For me, I learnt that the easy and fun way which was the direction these skydiving 'friends' were bringing me, was not the way forward for me, but I think I learnt that a little too late.

Kieran had no time for the direction I had chosen, and perhaps he'd leaned a little too much towards one direction whilst I was probably leaning too much in the opposite direction; however his approach allowed him to achieve his goals, and despite doing 180 jumps, when I ask him today if he was fully satisfied he always says that he would love to have kept it up. I asked him recently why he didn't, and he gave me the answer that has been heard within groups of men for eons, and eons... 'I met a girl'. And yes, he did, and he married that girl and has two wonderful kids now, and fabulous memories of skydiving not only in Ireland but in other countries too.

Kieran remained focussed, and whilst he has many great characteristics which would make him a fantastic leader, such as courage, resilience, dedication, and focus, he is a solo pilot, and unless his team was just him he'd struggle with the people management side of things. Kieran always liked to do everything himself, as he is such a perfectionist (well obviously except for driving to Magaluf), and as we all should know that's not possible when leading a team for so many reasons.

Throughout Kieran's progression the dreaded green-eyed monster used to raise its head a little amongst the rest of us. Despite us not doing anything really to improve ourselves, it was easy to pick holes in what Kieran was doing. 'Kieran and his new mates', 'he's one of them now', and many other things were mentioned about him whilst he was doing his thing. And what I most admire about him nowadays, and I wish I had been mature enough to realise it back then, he didn't give a shit what others thought about him. He was there to do what he needed to do, and he did it.

In those days I was so concerned about what others thought of me – I always wanted to impress people and sometimes I'd find that I'd alter my entire persona to try to fit in with others, and effectively become a whole different person. I think it's a trap that we all fall into at some stage in our lives, and it's a revelation, almost an epiphany, when you manage to release yourself from this mindset. It's important that you are respected and loved by those around you, and by those who care about you, but not everyone does, and once you escape that burden of expecting everyone to accept, respect, and love you, you free yourself from unnecessary stress. Who cares if your car isn't the nicest one on the street? Who cares if you don't keep up with the neighbours? The truly important people in your life won't care. I heard a celebrity once say, 'If you've a problem with me, just call me or text me. If you don't have my number, you don't know me well enough to have a problem with me'.

For such a young man to say such a thing is refreshing, and it's simple: filter out the noise and care about the people who care about you. Focus on what's important to your current or life objectives without neglecting those who are important to you and be kind along the way. It starts with you. Respect yourself regardless of your faults and flaws. And if you want respect and love, you need to give it first where it's due. Take time to be silent, for in the quiet moments you can sort things out and learn what's truly important.

Leadership Lesson – It's Not About Being Liked, It's About Being Respected

Paying too much attention to what others think, and worrying about whether your team likes you, can significantly affect both leaders and individuals in everyday life. Understanding that not everyone will like you is an important realisation that can impact how one manages relationships and expectations. For me, the moment I realised this, it felt like a weight had been lifted. Honestly, if you take only one thing from this book, please let it be this.

Here's a breakdown of the pros and cons of this dynamic:

Pros

- **Increased Empathy and Awareness:**
  Leaders who are attentive to others' opinions are often more empathetic and aware of how their actions affect those around them. This can lead to a more inclusive and considerate leadership style. But just because someone has an opinion, doesn't mean you must abide by it. Consider all input and make decisions based on what's best for the group or company as well as taking a look at refining or changing your leadership style if you feel it would grow or improve your awareness.

- **Improved Social Skills:**
  Paying attention to others' perceptions can enhance one's social skills, making it easier to navigate complex social situations and build relationships.

- **Adaptability:**
  Being receptive to feedback and understanding how you are perceived can help individuals adapt their behaviour in ways that are more likely to achieve desired outcomes, whether in leadership, teamwork, or personal interactions.

- **Continuous Improvement:**
  Constructive criticism is valuable for growth. Leaders who listen to feedback have the opportunity to continually improve their strategies, behaviours, and decision-making processes.

Cons

- **Over-Reliance on Approval:**
  Relying too heavily on others' approval can lead to a loss of authenticity. Leaders may become so concerned with pleasing others that they stray from their values and vision.

- **Decreased Decision-Making Confidence:**
  Constantly worrying about what others think can erode self-confidence. This may result in leaders who are less decisive, fearing criticism regardless of what choices they make.

- **Stress and Anxiety:**
  Over-concern with others' opinions can lead to increased stress and anxiety. Worrying about being liked or accepted can take a mental and emotional toll, affecting overall well-being.

- **Compromised Leadership Effectiveness:**
  Leaders who try too hard to be liked may struggle to enforce necessary but unpopular decisions. This can undermine their effectiveness and the respect they command from their team.

- **Dilution of Personal Identity:**
  In extreme cases individuals may alter their personalities or suppress their true selves to fit into perceived social norms, leading to dissatisfaction and loss of personal identity.

Understanding that not everyone will like you can be liberating and beneficial in several ways:

- **Freedom to Be Authentic:**
  Realising you can't please everyone frees you from the constraints of others' expectations, allowing you to be more authentic in your decisions and actions.

- **Improved Focus:**
  Leaders can focus more on what matters, achieving results and adhering to their vision rather than getting sidetracked by trying to win universal approval.

- **Resilience:**
  Developing a thicker skin in the face of criticism or disapproval helps build resilience, an essential trait for effective leadership and personal growth. Just don't let that thick skin blind you to what might be legitimate concerns presented by your team.

- **Better Resource Allocation:**
  By not expending energy on winning over every critic, leaders and individuals can more effectively allocate their efforts towards productive activities.

For leaders and individuals alike striking a balance between considering others' opinions and maintaining one's own convictions is key. It ensures that feedback is used constructively without compromising one's core identity or effectiveness.

Kieran would never let what other people thought about him get in his way. For our group he was an inspiration in this way, however, at the time, we never realised this. Instead his progression and steely focus would lead to some bitterness and resentment from some of us. Certainly, from my point of view, I didn't like the way that he was casting us aside and spending so much time with the other more qualified members of the club. I, more importantly, didn't like the way that he was learning so much and so fast. But rather than do something about it, I spent my time criticising him like a jealous little schoolboy. And not only that I also feel that I dragged my friend Sean into this behaviour as well, and that was reprehensible behaviour on my part.

Rather than us getting off our lazy backsides and learning a thing or two, we would rather sit together and bitch about him behind his back. I don't know if he ever knew we were doing that, but it was mean, hurtful, and showed disloyalty and disrespect for our friend who was pursuing and achieving what we all 'thought' we wanted.

Throughout our entire journey Kieran was always a couple of steps ahead of us, and despite us not even trying to keep up, we tried to take the goodness of all of his hard work away from him and belittle him. We were constantly doing it, and never once did we have the balls to say it to his face. And here's the reason why – it was rubbish. What on earth were we going to say?

'You're so good at what you're doing'.
'Another little gold star for the best pupil'.
'Aren't you so clever?'

Obviously, all said in the pitch of a sarcastic little 7-year-old kid, like a jealous bully. He could have answered all of those comments with a confident 'Yes', because the truth was that he was a star pupil who was doing so well. But we were childish and bitter and never ending.

It's so important to run your own race and ensure that you look at your own failings first before casting dispersions onto others. We were failing in our own goals, and rather than improving ourselves we belittled him.

Leadership Lesson – The Dangers of Disrespecting Others

When leaders or individuals focus on belittling others who are perceived as more successful or competent, rather than focusing on their own self-improvement, it can have detrimental effects on both their personal development and the environment around them. Here are some of the key consequences:

Impact on Personal Growth

- **Stagnation in Development:**
  By focusing on bringing others down instead of improving their own skills and abilities, individuals limit their growth and demoralise those around them. They miss out on learning opportunities and fail to develop the competencies that could enhance their personal and professional lives.

- **Reputation Damage:**
  Engaging in such negative behaviours can tarnish a person's reputation. Being known for negativity rather than positivity or competence can hinder career advancement and lead to social isolation.

- **Loss of Respect and Trust:**
  Peers, subordinates, and superiors often lose respect for those who consistently undermine others. This loss of respect can lead to decreased influence and a weakened ability to lead or collaborate effectively.

Impact on the Work Environment

- **Toxic Work Culture:**
  If a leader belittles others it can foster a toxic work environment that will spread, leading to a workplace culture where backstabbing, gossip,

and negativity are the norms rather than cooperation and mutual respect.

- **Lowered Team Morale and Motivation:**
  Team members are likely to feel demoralized and less motivated when they see others being unfairly criticised or belittled. This can lead to lower productivity and higher turnover rates.

- **Inhibition of Collaboration and Innovation:**
  An environment where individuals feel threatened or demeaned is not conducive to open communication and collaboration. This atmosphere stifles creativity and innovation because team members may be reluctant to share ideas for fear of being criticised or belittled.

Long-Term Consequences

- **Leadership Failure:**
  Leaders who engage in demeaning others may find themselves increasingly isolated. Over time their ability to lead effectively is compromised as they are unable to rally their teams or inspire loyalty.

- **Loss of Opportunities:**
  For individuals a reputation for negativity can close doors to new opportunities. Others may be reluctant to engage with someone known for belittling successful people, fearing similar treatment.

- **Legal and Ethical Repercussions:**
  In some cases persistent negative behaviour towards others can lead to formal complaints, legal action, and other serious consequences, especially if the behaviour crosses into harassment or discrimination.

Psychological Impact

- **Internal Conflict:**
  People who focus on undermining others often experience internal conflicts. Their actions may stem from insecurities or personal dissatisfaction, which can lead to further psychological distress.

- **Erosion of Self-Identity:**
  Over time individuals may come to define themselves more by their opposition to others than by their own positive qualities or achievements. This shift can erode self-identity and self-esteem.

The realisation of these impacts highlights the importance of focusing on personal growth and positive engagement with others. Leaders and individuals alike are better served by cultivating a supportive environment that encourages mutual improvement and celebrates collective success, rather than diminishing the accomplishments of others.

Sean and I had some serious issues with ourselves, and our insecurities and we needed to change, which I'm delighted to say we have, but not before we had done some damage in our relationships with others. And this damage took a period of time to repair. Funnily enough, I learned Kieran was oblivious to all of it as this behaviour was mainly conducted behind his back; however, the fallout from our other friends who would sometimes have to listen to us was very damaging.

Just a thought: if you're so worried about what other people think about you, and you're spending your time belittling and saying negative things about those who are doing well rather than improving yourself, I'll save you some time; this is what others think of you... they think you're a dick, and what's worse is they're right.

Nobody wants to sit in the company of someone who is constantly belittling others, is so negative about everything or is always looking for something or someone to blame. Seriously, life is too short, and it you've nothing positive to say, keep your mouth shut; you'll thank me for this piece of advice at some point in your life. Nobody likes it when others bring them down. And if that's you or you think that it might be, try to remember when you've sat in someone else's company who behaved like that and remember how you felt – yeah, it's not nice, right? And if they're talking that way about someone to you, you can be sure they'll be talking about you to someone else.

We really weren't nice people back then, and as I reflect on it, whenever we would leave the group, I now know what would have been said as we left – 'Thank Jaysus they're gone... don't think I could have listened to anymore of that shite any longer'.

Leadership Lesson – Take Ownership of every Aspect

Every scenario you encounter in your journey as a leader needs careful consideration and self-awareness. It's easy to pass the blame onto another person or area, however if you are the leader of this team, every aspect of the team and its performance is your responsibility and reflects on you.

In larger organisations there are HR teams who are supposed to deal with all the HR issues, there are training teams who are supposed to look after all of the training issues, but it is down to you to ensure that your team is catered for. Do not rely on HR or anyone else. The bottom line is, don't blame others when things don't go the way you want them to.

Taking ownership of every aspect of their team's issues is a fundamental aspect of effective leadership. While departments like Human Resources (HR) and Training are critical support systems within an organisation, leaders who proactively manage and take responsibility for their teams can drive better results and foster a more cohesive and productive environment. Here's a breakdown of why this approach is important:

Direct Impact on Team Dynamics and Performance

- **Immediate Problem Resolution:**
  Leaders who take direct ownership can address issues more swiftly and effectively. They are closer to the specific challenges their team faces and can implement targeted solutions without the delays that might occur when multiple departments are involved.

- **Increased Accountability:**
  When leaders take responsibility for all aspects of their team's functioning it sets a standard of accountability for the rest of the team. This can lead to higher levels of personal responsibility among team members as they follow the example set by their leader.

- **Better Understanding of Team Needs:**
  By engaging directly with their team's issues leaders gain a deeper understanding of the individual and collective needs of their team members. This insight allows for more effective management and the ability to advocate for resources or changes that will benefit the team.

Enhanced Communication and Relationships

- **Stronger Relationships:**
  Leaders who are actively involved can build stronger, more trusting relationships with their team members. These relationships are crucial

for maintaining loyalty, morale and motivation, especially during challenging times.

- **Clear Communication:**
  Direct involvement allows leaders to communicate expectations, feedback, and changes more clearly and directly. This reduces the risk of misunderstandings that can occur when messages are relayed through multiple parties.

Organisational Alignment and Efficiency

- **Alignment with Broader Goals:**
  Leaders who take comprehensive ownership ensure that their team's efforts are closely aligned with the organisation's goals. They can adjust more quickly in response to shifts in organisational priorities or market conditions.

- **Efficient Use of Resources:**
  By managing issues internally within the team leaders can make more efficient use of both human and material resources. This avoids the inefficiencies that can arise from involving multiple departments, which may not be as intimately familiar with the specific context or needs of the team.

Professional Growth and Team Development

- **Skill Development:**
  Leaders who actively manage their team's challenges develop a broader set of skills, including problem-solving, conflict resolution, and strategic thinking. These skills are critical for higher-level leadership roles.

- **Empowered Teams:**
  Teams led by a leader who takes full ownership are typically more empowered and autonomous. They benefit from clear direction and

support, while also being encouraged to develop their problem-solving capabilities.

Caveats and Considerations

While taking ownership is crucial leaders should also recognise the value of collaboration with specialised departments like HR and Training:

- **Leveraging Expertise:**
  HR and Training departments have specific expertise that can be vital in handling complex issues such as legal concerns, compliance, specialized training, and development programs. Leaders should know when to leverage this expertise to complement their leadership.

- **Avoiding Overload:**
  Leaders must avoid taking on so much that they become overwhelmed and unable to manage effectively. Delegation is a key leadership skill; knowing when and how to involve other departments strategically can enhance team management. Remember, delegation is not just downwards facing – it's sideways and upwards too.

In sum, while support departments are essential, the direct involvement of a leader in all facets of team management is critical for driving team success, ensuring effective problem resolution, and fostering a productive and positive work environment. This approach not only enhances team operations but also contributes significantly to the leader's growth and development.

In a past life, whilst working as a leader in a financial services organisation, I constantly found myself disagreeing with the HR team. Not that the HR team were wrong, but just that their advice was affecting the efficiencies and productivity of my team. I realised that I wasn't educated enough to have these discussions, so I enrolled in Employment Law in the Law

Society of Ireland, and my mind opened dramatically. If there is an area of a business that you don't understand, learn about it.

This will broaden your horizons and help you in your goal to achieve higher levels of leadership. Smaller organisations, in my opinion, are great places to start your leadership career because you get the opportunity to wear every hat and learn more about the entire organisation and its various functions because you have to, as there's nobody else there to do it. Sometimes in larger organisations, your learnings can be stifled due to the structures in place.

This is not to say that you *must* deal with everything yourself, but you should have the knowledge so that you can respond effectively and efficiently and lean on those around you for advice and guidance as required. If you are in a predicament that is over your head, always reach out and seek help and support.

Kieran eventually bought his own parachute, which I think cost him about €2,000 - an extremely expensive purchase for us at that time. He travelled to so many different countries skydiving in each and had a wonderful career until, as previously mentioned, he found the girl of his dreams. I often regret that my actions may have prevented him from living this life, a life that I had truly wanted for myself, and I admire him for being able to push all of the noise away and concentrate on what was important to him and achieving his goals. I truly learnt so much more from him in this time that I could ever imagine learning in an organisation and I thank him for his patience and forgiveness. We are still good friends to this day, and even still I find myself having to hold back the green-eyed monster every now and then when he displays his fortitude, resilience and determination.

When he eventually left the club, he didn't mean to leave it for good and he lent his parachute to another skydiver asking him to look after it for him. I don't think he ever got it back. Despite all of his wonderful characteristics and how he always thought so well of others, I'd have seen that coming a mile away! Sucker!! (Sorry Kieran, couldn't help myself). As I'm writing this segment, I'm wondering if Kieran, with all of his insight and ability to move in the right direction, didn't purposely and knowingly give his parachute to someone he knew could make good use of it, fully knowing he would never get it back, and perhaps doing it because he didn't want to be tempted away from his new life.

CHAPTER 13

THE INCIDENT

As previously mentioned, one of our friends was awarded the nickname 'Dead Man Walking'; that friend was Sean. And this is his story.

It was my 8 second freefall, not too sure how high Kieran was going, and it was Sean's 5 second freefall. After weeks of him being away from the club I had convinced Sean that his nerves were purely down to the lack of momentum and that once he jumps back on the horse we could continue to journey to the top of the skies. There was also the fact that on Sean's first freefall jump the instructors had marked that jump in his logbook as 'text book'; despite the failings of his previous training jumps, this comment gave Sean the added confidence that he knew what he was doing, and that he'd do the next one in a 'text book' manner too.

We couldn't allow Kieran to get the better of us; we needed to prove that we were just as good. It took a few nights in our local pub to convince him, but he came in eventually, and here we were again lifting off from a cold airfield in Clonbullogue in County Offaly.

Kieran was at the back of the plane; I was in the middle and Sean was closest to the door. This was due to the different heights we were jumping from; Sean was 3,000 feet, me at 3,500 feet and Kieran a good bit higher. It was great having the three of us in the plane together; we sometimes had been separated on previous jumps, and despite all of our bitching about Kieran, it really was great to be doing this together again.

We had such a laugh on the way up and the slagging was immense. Sean was a little quiet, but we put that down to nerves and because he had been away from jumping for a little while.

Sean's journey thus far had been littered with mistakes, mishaps, and refused jumps. And when I say refused jumps, I mean that the club refused to allow him to jump due to heavy nights of drinking the night before and not being in a fit enough state. They were a very safety focussed club, as you would hope and expect them to be, and the slightest hint that somebody wasn't fully fit would be enough for them to ground you.

Sean's skydiving attire was slightly different to everyone else – he wore George Webb hard soled shoes, white socks, and what he would refer to as his 'night' jeans. Sean packed lightly. He would have one pair of shoes for whatever he was doing, he would have two pairs of jeans, one for daytime and going out in the evening, and another for wearing in bed (yes, I know) and for skydiving. Again, yes, I know. The rest of us would wear soft soled runners, or trainers, usually not in the best of condition as there was high likelihood of landing in sheep shit or even worse, and either light trousers, sometimes tracksuits and sometimes jeans depending on the temperature. It was always cold at altitude but a lot of times you didn't feel that cold; it was more the temperature on the ground that we paid attention to. The reason for the runners or trainers was to have a bit of grip when coming in to land.

Sean's landings were a spectacle to see. Every landing was a sliding landing – it was like someone had always left a skateboard at exactly the right spot for him to land on and it took him another 30 yards down the field. He usually ended up on his arse. We used to always laugh about how his shoes were always so well polished when we arrived at the club, and within an hour or two, they were caked in shit – he didn't care. Moreover, his night jeans were spotless on arrival but not for long. If he managed to jump on the Saturday, it meant that he would go to bed that night in the state they had become during the day. It was so funny to see him at the B&B at the end of a Saturday's jumping, changing into his day jeans to go to the pub, and then back into the filthy night jeans for a drunken night's sleep – each to their own as they say. Obviously if there was no jumping on a Saturday due to the weather Sean would be spotless for the entire 24 hours.

As we got to the right altitude for Sean to jump the door opened and the instructor stuck his head out to get the right spot. Usually this was simple – the instructor would look directly down, find the appropriate spot by directing the pilot and then call to the pilot to throttle down the engines and go into a glide. The first jumper would shuffle up to the door, exit the plane, the instructor would give the thumbs up or some other form of telling you to get the hell off the plane (they were quite imaginative the better they knew you), and they would watch you fall as you completed your count and your parachute opened. Usually the others in the plane would count at the same time, as it was quite natural to do, and once the count was complete the instructor would pull the door closed, signal to the pilot to throttle up the engines and look back at the others in the plane to say either, 'Great job' or 'Made a balls of that', or whatever – there was always a comment or a smirk or a funny quip. Some people would accidentally do a tumble and get an immediate fail (it was great craic in fairness), but the quip was usually, 'Arse over tit – has to do it again'.

This time was a first for both Kieran and me. As Sean climbed out we shouted, 'Break a leg, mate', and on signal he was gone. We both started counting out loud – generally you'd keep this count to yourself as you may not have known the others in the plane too well, but because it was us, and we were friends, we did it together - one one thousand, two one thousand, three one thousand, four one thousand, five one thousand... the instructors head was still sticking out the door. Six one thousand, seven one thousand, eight one thousand, and no sign of it coming back in. Kieran and I both stared at each other. What was going wrong? We couldn't see what was happening below. Neither could we stand up to look out the window as that was against the rules and would obviously have disrupted the balance of the plane – these are small planes – nine one thousand, ten one thousand, eleven one thousand... still no movement from the instructor as he was glued to the proceeding below him in the sky.

The ground comes up very fast the longer you fall. As the speed of your fall increases to a maximum velocity, which is 120mph, the first thousand feet takes about 10 seconds to complete and each following 1,000 feet whilst at maximum velocity takes only 5 seconds. The plan for Sean's jump was that he would let go of the plane at 3,000 feet, freefall for 5 seconds allowing him plenty of sky below him to safely open his parachute after a fall of 500 feet and 2,500 feet. After eleven seconds - eleven one thousand - Sean was now below 2,000 feet and falling at maximum velocity. Every second he fell another 200 feet, which meant only 10 seconds until impact, or as they would say in skydiving circles, bouncing. We didn't need to have calculators to figure this out – with the relatively little experience both myself and Kieran had accumulated we just knew this. What was going on?

Bouncing? What an expression to use in this environment. I'm not sure how much bouncing you'd do if you found yourself in this predicament. The fields below, although luscious with beautiful green grass, weren't made from trampolines and didn't have much give in them. There were also very few trees in the area. It's said, and this is not a recommendation, that if your parachute doesn't open, and your reserve doesn't deploy, aim for the trees to help break your fall. Easy to say if there are trees nearby, but generally skydivers only attempt to open their parachutes at 2,000, which is realistically 10 seconds until 'bouncing', so looking for a lovely patch of trees and redirecting yourself at this stage is probably futile, unless you're lucky enough to have been falling directly above some. The rules of the Irish Parachute Club back in those days said that no parachutes were to be deployed under 2,000 feet. Sean was now, according to our count, at approx. 1,800 feet.

Twelve one thousand, thirteen one thousand, fourteen one thousand. Neither of us knew what was going on and couldn't even speak. We were both thinking the worst and we both knew that it was a real possibility. The door slammed shut; the instructor turned to the pilot slightly panicked and told him to restart the engines. No glance back... no, 'Great job' or 'Made a balls of that' or even 'Arse over tit', although that would have probably been the most appropriate comment.

'What happened', we asked, and no response. We asked again. 'Don't worry about it lads... just keep focused' – that was probably the worst thing to say to us and brought an instant fear of the unknown over us. It's funny... even at this time I couldn't wait to get out of the plane. I needed to see what was going on and what had happened. It never even once crossed my mind that whatever had happened to Sean would happen to me – I didn't know what had happened to Sean, and maybe that's exactly what the instructor was keeping from us. I had to get out to see for myself.

We reached 3,500 feet and it was my turn.

The fear of the unknown can also affect those of you in leadership but let's discuss this at the end of this story, as it's getting good now (finally, says you).

We reached 3,500 feet and it was my turn. The door opened and you couldn't have kept me in the plane – I needed to know if Sean was ok and I needed to get to him. As I swung my legs out, I said to the instructor, 'I'm just going'. He nodded in agreement, I grabbed the strut with one hand, placed one foot on the wheel, reached out to the strut with my other hand, and before I had pulled my leg from inside the plane, I let go. It was only an 8 second freefall, so I continued with my count, ensured I was stable, and deployed my parachute. When it opened, I looked down immediately and saw Sean lying on the ground spread eagled, like a human 'X', and people were running out across the fields from the hanger to where he was. Nobody had reached him at this stage and they were all probably 200 feet, if not more, away from where he lay. I knew I needed to get down quickly – I'm not sure why, because if he'd bounced, it really didn't matter how fast or slow I got there, but I never thought about it like that. I needed to get to my friend and see how he was. I completed my checks, released my toggles and then from 2,500 feet I pulled down hard on one toggle, placing the parachute into a circular spin, or a spiral, which would allow me to get down as fast as possible (obviously there's a quicker way, but I wanted to get down alive). As I was getting dizzier and dizzier, the ground approached me quite quickly. I knew the club's rules about not spiralling below 1,000 feet, but I made a conscious, and extremely irresponsible decision to disregard those rules and try to get to my friend as quickly as possible. That was my only priority, and in hindsight, it was foolish. The parachute was swinging my legs out practically sideways at this stage and I hurtled towards the ground. At about 150 feet I levelled up into the wind and came into land approximately 40 feet from where Sean was. While I was in the spiral two of the people running out from the hanger spotted me and broke away from the group and came to help me with the landing. Only writing this now I wonder if they thought that there was something wrong with my parachute by the way I was descending, and that's why they came to help, but I never asked and they never said.

While writing this book, I spoke to a member of the club, told him this story and he confirmed that that would have been exactly what was assumed. Although all I cared about was getting to my friend, my actions caused others to focus their attention on me, while their attention should have remained solely on Sean. Again, another selfish act without thought of consequence.

As I landed they grabbed my lines, helped deflate the parachute, I jumped from the harness leaving it with them and ran to Sean. The others were there now and I ran through the group of them. There Sean lay, face up, eyes closed. He looked like he was in one piece, but he wasn't moving. 'Sean', I said. 'You ok?' And with that he opened his eyes, and his exact words were, 'Holy shit, I'm alive'.

It was such a relief to see he was alive – I had no idea what had happened, but something went wrong and it wasn't just from the long count I saw in the plane or just from the gang of people running out from the hanger I saw while under canopy or even just the rig that was surrounding Sean on the ground – it was combination of everything. The rig was especially unusual...both parachutes had been deployed...his main chute, and his reserve chute. Initially I couldn't tell which was which, but one of them was still in the bag and hadn't opened.

I had previously mentioned about how a parachute opens but I'll remind you. If you don't need reminding, skip the next section.

A parachute opens through a controlled process that starts when the parachute is deployed from its pack:

- **Deployment:** The process begins when the skydiver pulls the deployment handle attached to the pilot chute, a small auxiliary parachute. This action releases the pilot chute into the airstream.

- **Pilot Chute Inflation:** Once released, the pilot chute catches the air and inflates. Its main function is to create drag, pulling the deployment bag (containing the main parachute) out of the backpack container.

- **Line Stretch:** As the deployment bag is pulled away by the pilot chute, the suspension lines of the parachute (which connect the parachute to the skydiver's harness) are extracted and stretched out. This helps to ensure that the parachute will unfold in an orderly manner.

- **Canopy Extraction:** After the lines are stretched, the deployment bag opens (usually the bag is closed during packing using elastic bands, commonly referred to as 'bungees'), allowing the canopy (the main part of the parachute) to start to unfurl and catch air.

- **Canopy Inflation:** The canopy of the parachute begins to inflate gradually, usually starting from the centre and moving outward. This happens as the air fills the cells of the parachute through openings at the front.

- **Fully Open Parachute:** As the canopy inflates it slows the skydiver's descent. The entire process from pulling the pilot chute to having a fully inflated parachute typically takes just a few seconds.

As Sean became a little more coherent and sat up from the ground, thankfully with no injuries, one of the most senior members of the club, the person who has specific responsibility for the packing of reserve parachutes, went to the unopened bag, gave the lines a slight pull and the bungees released. The parachute fell out onto the ground. 'How did that not open?' he exclaimed, and that was when I realised it was the reserve in the bag.

So now it got really confusing. How is someone on the ground safely with a released reserve chute which didn't deploy, and a fully deployed main parachute. The only time a reserve chute is used is when the main chute either doesn't open or malfunctions but, in this scenario, the main chute had deployed and was fully functional and the reserve chute had also been deployed but was still in the bag. If that bag had opened during the canopy ride, it could have entangled with the main chute and both could have been compromised. That could have ended in disaster. And by the look of it, all it took was a slight pull and it opened.

What in hell had happened up there? We would have to wait until Sean got himself together again and let him tell us what happened. The first thing was to get him back to the hanger and check that he was physically ok.

That was Sean's 21st jump and there would never be a 22nd. He was physically ok but he was shaken, and it took some time for him to come out of that. He didn't want to go to the hospital to be checked out, all he wanted to do was, 'Let's just go for a pint', and so we did. It was mid-afternoon and we all packed up for the day. The majority of the members of the club went to the pub to find out what had happened. I was the stupid one to suggest that he go straight back up again rather than go to the pub because, as I'd said, 'If you don't do it now, you never will again'. His response was clear, concise and fully understood: 'Yeah right... pint please'. 'I don't know what you've just been through but your wish is our command', and off we went.

Before I go into Sean's story further, and how he managed to find himself in this situation (and survive), let's just quickly back track to the fear we experienced in the plane of not knowing what had happened. We had obviously assumed the worst, and why wouldn't we? We were not aware of other outcomes available at this time. Our limited experience in skydiving taught us that everything goes to plan or you die.

Leadership Lesson – Opening Your Mind

However, that's very shortsighted and there are always other outcomes, as we found out. When under pressure, our minds instantly and reactively jump to what we know and what our experience has taught us but from this day onwards, I knew and learnt that anything is possible and not to always jump to a restricted assumption.

Never try to restrict your imagination and your problem solving to what is currently within your head, rather open your mind and don't make rash assumptions before having time to understand information that perhaps you have not yet become acquainted with.

'The oldest and strongest emotion of mankind is fear, and the oldest and strongest kind of fear is the fear of the unknown'.

– H.P. Lovecraft (American Author)

Dealing with the fear of the unknown is a significant challenge for leaders in various contexts, from business uncertainty to navigating organisational change. Here's a breakdown of the difficulties and some strategies for managing this fear:

Difficulties for Leaders

- **Uncertainty Impact:**
  Leaders must often make decisions with incomplete information as we had done in the plane. This can lead to second-guessing and stress as

they weigh potential outcomes, knowing that their choices can significantly impact their organisation and its people.

- **Maintaining Team Morale:**
  The fear of the unknown can trickle down from leadership to employees, creating a work environment filled with anxiety and decreased productivity. Leaders need to manage not only their own fears but also reassure their team and maintain morale.

- **Communication Challenges:**
  Effective communication becomes particularly challenging when future conditions are uncertain. Leaders must decide how much to share and in what manner, balancing transparency with the need to avoid creating unnecessary panic.

- **Risk Management:**
  Leaders must navigate through risks without always knowing which risks are worth taking. This can make it challenging to strategically plan and prioritize resources effectively.

- **Personal Stress and Resilience:**
  Leaders are also human and may struggle with their own fears and uncertainties while needing to appear confident and decisive. This can lead to burnout and decision fatigue.

Tips for Managing Fear of the Unknown

- **Foster a Culture of Openness:**
  Encourage a culture where team members feel safe discussing their fears and uncertainties. This can lead to shared solutions and decrease the feeling of isolation.

- **Focus on Controllable Elements:**
  While it's impossible to control everything, leaders can focus on areas where they can make a difference. Identifying what can be controlled and taking action there can provide a sense of security and accomplishment.

- **Increase Flexibility in Planning:**
  Adopt flexible strategies that allow for adjustments as new information becomes available. This could involve scenario planning and developing contingency plans.

- **Communicate Effectively and Often:**
  Provide regular updates to keep the team informed, even if the update is to confirm that uncertainty remains. Transparency builds trust and can help mitigate fears.

- **Seek External Advice:**
  When dealing with unprecedented situations, consulting with mentors, peers, or industry experts can provide new perspectives and reduce the feeling of going it alone.

- **Prioritise Personal and Team Resilience:**
  Invest in resilience-building activities for the team and personal wellness for leaders. This could include training, workshops, and ensuring that workloads are manageable.

- **Embrace Continuous Learning:**
  Encourage a learning mindset that views challenges as opportunities to grow and learn. This can transform fear into curiosity and proactive problem-solving.

By acknowledging the fear of the unknown and implementing these strategies, leaders can better navigate uncertain waters, making informed decisions and maintaining a supportive, productive work environment.

In a lot of change management scenarios this is the number one factor for resistance from other stakeholders. All change management trainings will teach you to ensure you communicate the upcoming changes to everyone who would be affected, however, whilst I fully agree with that philosophy, in certain scenarios where the apprehension and anxiety of the upcoming change may be more damaging than the change itself, it can be equally important to keep a few things on your chest, rather than offloading them to unsuspecting team members.

A key strength for any leader these days, whether it be about maintaining motivation, ensuring employee engagement or managing upcoming changes, is positivity. And that being said, positivity is not enough on its own; a truly great leader needs to be consistently positive. I'll say that again; a truly great leader needs to be consistently positive.

A leader's positivity is crucial in managing a team effectively. It sets the tone of the work environment, influences the team's morale, and can significantly impact productivity and cohesion. Here's why a consistently positive attitude is vital for leadership:

- **Enhancing Team Morale:**
  Positive leaders tend to create an optimistic and encouraging atmosphere that can enhance team morale. A high morale often leads to increased job satisfaction, lower turnover rates, greater loyalty to the company mission and its leaders, and enhanced creativity and innovation.

- **Boosting Productivity:**
  Leaders who approach challenges with a positive attitude can inspire their team to tackle their tasks more confidently and creatively. This can lead to higher productivity and better problem-solving.

- **Improving Communication:**
  Positivity promotes open communication. Teams are more likely to share ideas, voice concerns, and collaborate effectively when they feel supported by an upbeat, aware, and open-minded leader.

- **Fostering Resilience:**
  By maintaining a positive outlook leaders can help their teams navigate through failures or tough times, encouraging resilience and a focus on growth and learning from experiences.

- **Attracting and Retaining Top Talent:**
  Talented individuals are drawn to environments where they feel valued and positive. Leaders who exude positivity help in not just attracting but also retaining top talent.

Tips for Managing Consistent Positivity

- **Practice Self-awareness:**
  Leaders should cultivate self-awareness to recognise their emotional states and understand how their moods and attitudes affect others. Reflecting on one's impact can guide a leader to adjust their approach to be more positively perceived.

- **Set a Positive Example:**
  Actions speak louder than words. By demonstrating positivity in their own behaviour — such as focusing on solutions rather than problems — leaders can directly influence their team's mindset.

- **Encourage Open Communication:**
  Foster an environment where team members feel comfortable expressing their thoughts and feelings. This openness can prevent misunderstandings and build mutual trust.

- **Recognise and Celebrate Successes:**
  Regularly acknowledging individual and team achievements can boost morale and reinforce a positive environment. This could be as simple as a shout-out in a meeting or they can be in the form of more formal rewards.

- **Maintain a Healthy Work-Life Balance:**
  Leaders should advocate for and model a healthy balance between work and personal life. Respecting personal boundaries and promoting well-being can help maintain a positive team spirit.

- **Provide Support and Training:**
  Equip your team with the necessary resources and training to succeed. Supportive leaders are seen as positive forces in the workplace, enhancing team confidence and capabilities.

- **Stay Constructively Optimistic:**
  While positivity is key it's also important to stay realistic. Address challenges openly but focus on constructive ways to overcome them, showing confidence in your team's abilities.

By integrating these strategies, leaders can not only enhance their own positivity but also instil it within their teams, leading to a more motivated, engaged, and productive workforce.

Now, back to Sean. This is what happened as told by Sean from his own perspective. We sat in the pub listening to what Sean had to tell us, and there were lessons for all of us. It wasn't just on him where the blame lay, it was also us and the club itself. I've often thought that one of the most valuable things to have come out of Sean's survival, other than obviously him still being alive, is the fact that he *was* still alive and able to teach us all a valuable lesson.

By absolutely no means did Sean place the blame towards anybody but himself, and to be honest, he probably never even thought like that; but it was clear to everyone who he told his story to that night that the blame was clearly shared, and we were all responsible.

At the very beginning, Sean never really wanted to do a jump, not even the tandem, but he suffered from the fear of missing out. He was terrified to jump but he didn't know enough to justify that fear, so he gave it a go and did the tandem. Once the rest of us said that we were going to continue (again, Sean had been content with what he'd already achieved), between the peer pressure placed on him by the rest of us and the thought of being the only one left in Dublin while the rest of us were at the club, which was not very appealing to him, he kept it up.

When we talk about the peer pressure at this level, although I think that you should never allow others to dictate your own actions, at this age it was extremely difficult to go against the rest of us. The first person to quit would have been deemed as the person who was, for want of a better phrase, 'chicken shit', and probably would never have lived it down, especially given our past history of the years of teasing we had been giving Kieran about taking that infamous left to Magaluf. As Sean said, it took less courage to jump out of the plane than to be that guy. Also, it was the fear of loneliness when the rest of us were at the club – he really just wanted to hang out with us; he once said, 'Wouldn't it have been great if you lads had just taken up fishing?', and somebody replied, 'But then you'd have just fallen in the river, and you can't swim... swings & roundabouts'.

In hindsight, the first person who gave up wasn't ostracised or ridiculed, in fact it was the opposite; it caused a little bit of a ripple and gave a viable option to others who were of the same mindset as Sean, but unfortunately at that time, Sean didn't walk through that door. When it was just the three of us left, we were all getting braver, including Sean, and we were getting better. Sean's experience however was not as consistent as Kieran's and mine, so his jumps weren't perfect, and he had to repeat a number of them.

The most enlightening and disturbing moment of Sean's story was when he told us about his progression through the DRP jumps, the static line jumps which required you to simulate pulling the ripcord. At no point during that progression did Sean manage to find the ripcord, yet he still progressed. While he was on the ground practising and lying with his belly down on a dolly, he would always reach it, and pull it successfully, but when he was in the air, and when he truly needed to reach it, he could never find it. Possibly because he only had three seconds to do so, and realistically it wasn't three seconds, it was on the third second that you reached down to find it, therefore you had only one chance before the static line opened the chute for you. At that stage it was too late.

On every jump, the instructor would look out the door to ensure you followed the motions, but it was too difficult for the instructor to see whether you had managed to reach the ripcord as you'd have been too far away from the plane to see. On the ground, the instructor there would watch you land, and that instructor would look out for one thing... had the ripcord been pulled, and where was it. We were told to just put it between our teeth because we would eventually need to use both our hands. Each time Sean landed, the ripcord was in his mouth. So from the instructor's view in the plane, Sean had performed the action of reaching for the ripcord; from the instructor's view on the ground, Sean had pulled the ripcord as it was in his mouth when he landed. From Sean's view while in the air, however, the parachute had opened already, he was safely floating through the air at 2,500 feet and he thought that he'd better pull the ripcord now or the instructor on the ground would fail him and it would slow his progression.

Let's just think about that for a moment!!

But in Sean's mind it was so important to keep up with the two of us that he was willing to disregard his own safety and 'fake it'. He just didn't want to be left behind.

Although he failed one of the DRP jumps, it wasn't because of missing the ripcord, it was for another stability issue – he never managed to reach the ripcord on any of his DRP jumps, and funnily enough he never thought it was going to be an issue because he never thought that they'd actually let him freefall if he wasn't able to open the parachute. And there was the gap that Sean had just slipped through.

Despite the stringent safety measures within the club, and despite stringent policies and procedures within businesses and organisations, people have to take responsibility for their own actions and cannot fully rely on others to manage that responsibility for them. People will always find a way to circumvent rules and regulations for whatever reasons – Sean's reasoning was that it didn't really matter as they'll finally spot what he was doing and stop him from doing freefall; but they didn't. It wouldn't be the first time that somebody did something that got them noticed. Sometimes it's only noticed after multiple occasions, and sometimes not at all.

When Sean was passed for freefall he never said a word to anyone, and the pressure on him was immense. He didn't want to risk falling behind Kieran and I and he didn't want to just quit, but this situation had grown from a simple problem to an elongated period of deception where he had hidden his true abilities (or lack thereof) from the club, and he most definitely didn't want to admit to that. He was running out of options. The responsible thing to do would have been to come clean, but he thought he could fix it himself, and took the biggest risk of his life – he did his 3 second freefall.

Remarkably, he did the best jump of his life. And he loved it. In hindsight as he told us, he loved it because he had survived a jump that, in his mind, he thought would have been the death of him – I can only imagine what was going through his head when he was preparing to jump out of the plane this time. Knowing that you had never managed to reach the ripcord in all of your practice jumps (DRPs), but still pushing yourself to jump when knowing this was the one time that you had to.

I asked him what he was thinking and he said that he always remembered his training of: if you can't get the main ripcord, pull the reserve (the reserve handle was located on your chest, so it was easier to get to). To this day, I cannot believe how someone could jump out of a plane thinking that pulling the reserve chute was a very viable option – it's supposed to be a last chance option. However, on his 3 second freefall, he didn't have to, thankfully. His first time reaching the ripcord was on his very first freefall, with no safety net (static line) to open his parachute for him and only his reserve as his back-up. Unbelievable.

So, hurry up buddy... what happened on the next one? Ok so...

After those weeks of persistence from me, Sean agreed to do his 5 second freefall, and you already know the build up to that.

Sean had this added confidence now that he'd done it on his last jump, so he felt that this was easy. When Sean left the plane, the luck he'd experienced in his previous jump left him, and he tried to reach his main ripcord, but couldn't. He did everything that he should have done and kept himself stable by pulling one hand down for the ripcord and the other hand across his head to maintain that stability. But he'd missed. So, he tried again, and panic crept in. This time, he only pulled his right hand down to pull the ripcord and left his other hand outstretched. This meant his body position was somewhat like John Travolta in Saturday Night Fever whilst strutting across the dancefloor. Great for the dancefloor, but not great for aerodynamic stability. He immediately went into a spin when the air grabbed a hold of his outstretched left arm and twisted him around. Due to this sudden change in positioning, he missed the main ripcord again and continued to plummet towards the ground, at this stage reaching terminal velocity. His training kicked in, and he went for the reserve handle which was on his chest.

The reserve chute is designed slightly differently to the main chute which just opens and releases the chute. The reserve chute is designed to propel the reserve chute away from the body and then deploy in case the skydiver is struggling to maintain stability. However, Sean was now in a desperate situation and was spinning uncontrollably in the sky. When he pulled the handle, the reserve chute tried to propel itself away from Sean but because he was spinning so fast, the lines wrapped themselves around his neck, and the back, which contained the parachute, didn't receive enough pressure on it to release the canopy. The only thing this managed to do was create a noose around Sean's neck as he continued to fall to earth.

As he fell, the unopened bag was being pulled behind him and danced back and forth above his head – if it had opened at this stage it would most definitely have instantly broken his neck. As he continued to fall and got even closer to the ground, again Sean's training kicked in and he remembered to arch his body to regain stability. He did what we had done so many times like idiots in the pub back then: he threw his arms and legs out into the sky and created a perfect 'x' shape, causing him to stabilise on his front, with the main parachute where it should be, facing the sky and not the ground. And now for the 50/50 chance.

The reserve chute was still dancing back and forth above him. If he pulled the main chute while the reserve bag was doing its backwards dance, the main chute would deploy directly into this bag, and it would have been game over – neither would open and he would 'bounce'. If he pulled the main chute while the reserve bag was doing its forwards dance, he had a chance but he still had to contend with the lines from the reserve chute being entangled around his neck. If his main chute opened successfully, and the sudden reduction in speed caused the reserve to open at the same time, again this could have broken his neck, and although he wouldn't have 'bounced', it would still have been game over.

Instead, the main chute opened at the right time avoiding the reserve chute, the reserve didn't open at all, and Sean landed in the soft grass after a canopy ride of less than 30 seconds – his main parachute was deployed at 900 feet, which if it hadn't would have given Sean only another 4 to 5 seconds to live. He never thought about timing the opening of the main parachute – he was just grateful that he found it when it really mattered.

Never before had the club ever seen a person make a successful landing after deploying a reserve chute before deploying the main chute – it just wasn't the order in which things were done. The risk affiliated with deploying a main chute whilst the reserve had been opened are so high as there is no way to release a reserve away from you before doing so – there is no release mechanism on a reserve chute as there would never be a reason to cut it away. The reserve chute is there to provide you with exactly what it's called – a reserve. Generally, if your main parachute doesn't open correctly, there are two handles on your chest – the one on the left releases the main parachute from your harness and allows it to float away into the sky so that it doesn't interfere with the opening of the reserve. The training tells you to pull down hard on the right handle, and then immediately afterwards, pull down hard on the left handle to deploy the reserve. This is for use 99.9999% of times, and normal procedure. Sean however didn't even listen to that part of the training and thankfully so.

Imagine this... falling through the sky at 120 mph, realising that you couldn't open your main parachute and going for your reserve. Imagine he had pulled down hard on the right handle, which at that time would have done nothing that he would have seen or felt, and then pulling down hard on the left handle which deployed the reserve that then wrapped around his neck. Now, if he had followed his training, and hadn't used his initiative, even at this level of crisis, what would have happened next would have been catastrophic. He would have finally managed to find the ripcord for his main parachute, he would have pulled it, but because he had already pulled down hard on the right handle to release this parachute from his harness, the bag containing the parachute would have just fallen away from his body and guess what...he'd have 'bounced'.

Not only was the training provided to us in such a manner that we knew what we needed to know, it was delivered in a manner that we understood it, so that if we needed to adjust and, as the Americans might say, 'call an audible', we understood why we were doing that. Sean understood very clearly even in the highest level of stress that he didn't need to and shouldn't pull the right handle – he went straight for the left, and ultimately that unconscious thinking and level of understanding saved his life.

Leadership Lesson – The Goal of Teaching is Always Understanding

It's the same in leadership. Sometimes the provision of a job spec to explain responsibilities or a training tick box exercise, which measures how many people have been taught rather than how many people have an understanding, can be very detrimental for a leader of a team. Sometimes the transition from teaching to understanding what has been taught falls directly onto your shoulders.

Understanding job requirements and receiving proper training are critical elements for any team's success.

For leaders, ensuring that their team members are well-versed in these areas is particularly important for several reasons:

- **Clarity in Roles and Responsibilities:**
  When team members understand their job requirements clearly, it minimises confusion and overlap of duties. This clarity helps in setting expectations and contributes to a more efficient and effective workflow.

- **Empowerment through Knowledge:**
  Proper training equips team members with the necessary skills and knowledge to perform their tasks effectively. When team members feel confident in their abilities, they are more likely to take initiative and make informed decisions independently. This is exactly what kept Sean alive – his understanding of how his rig worked.

- **Enhanced Decision-Making:**
  With a thorough understanding of their roles and the training to back up their skills, team members are better prepared to face unexpected situations. This ability to make informed decisions is crucial, especially when immediate guidance from leadership isn't available.

- **Increased Productivity:**
  Teams that understand their roles and are well-trained can work more autonomously, reducing the need for constant supervision. This not only boosts productivity but also allows leaders to focus on strategic aspects rather than micromanagement.

- **Improved Morale and Motivation:**
  Employees who feel competent and understand their job expectations are generally more satisfied and motivated. This positive attitude can lead to higher retention rates and a more harmonious workplace.

- **Risk Reduction:**
  Proper training and clear understanding of job duties can reduce errors and mishaps. This is particularly important in industries where errors can have significant financial or safety implications.

- **Adaptability and Innovation:**
  When team members are well-trained and clear about their roles, they are more likely to adapt to changes and contribute innovative ideas. This adaptability is key to maintaining competitiveness and responding effectively to industry changes or challenges.

By investing in the training and development of their teams, and ensuring that all members understand their specific roles, leaders can build a more resilient, efficient, and motivated workforce. This approach not only enhances individual performance but also drives the overall success of the organisation.

Sean told me much later that because the training he, and the rest of us, received had provided him with such an ingrained level of understanding of the workings of the parachute, prior to pulling the reserve he thought to himself, 'once I open this one, I'll release the main just in case. I don't want that to open by accident and become entangled in my reserve'. Obviously, he never needed to do that because the reserve had malfunctioned, but the thought process was there, and although very different in how we were taught, it was the right way of thinking. By Sean understanding the way the rig worked, and by the club ensuring that we had this understanding, and not just instruction, he was able to be creative in his actions and find solutions to problems which we weren't told about. In essence, this understanding saved his life.

Oh, and one last thing about this: not only can we attribute Sean's survival to his understanding of the workings of a parachute and the various ripcords and levers, there is also the small fact of the person who packed his main parachute, which saved his life when the reserve didn't open properly, despite the years and year of experience that the reserve chute packer had under his belt.

Sean was insistent about asking the club to check the logs to see who had packed the parachute that had saved his life. 'I owe this person everything, and I can at least buy whoever it was a pint'. Sean, Kieran and I were sitting around a table in the pub with so many other members of the club listening to Sean's story, when one of the others came in with the news of who was logged in as the person who packed that parachute. During the time we were sitting there, Kieran knew that it was him; he had recognised the rig while Sean was in the plane, but never said a word. He didn't know that Sean had asked the club to find out who had packed it, so when that person arrived and told Sean that it was one of his own friends who had saved his life that day, Sean instantly and most certainly knew that it wasn't me; it had to have been Kieran. I had been as lazy as him and hadn't bothered learning how to do it. And he knew that it was the very same Kieran who we had been speaking about behind his back for so long; the same Kieran who we had been jealous of and ridiculed his success for the past year or so; the same Kieran whose meticulous adherence to the rules and regulations, whose almost mechanical manner of progressing seamlessly through his journey making it look so simple, but doing so without bragging whilst being needlessly and unknowingly ridiculed by two 'jealous idiots'; the same Kieran who had just saved his life. And just to be sure, the guy from the club confirmed it was Kieran; just for a second I thought how cool it would be if he said my name, knowing full well that was impossible – but you know, such an arrogant selfish thought at such an inappropriate time!

Would I have taken the credit if they mistakenly called my name? Nowadays, most certainly not, but back then...I don't know. I'm pleased the person I was back then is firmly in the rear view mirror; I won't ever let myself forget him because that's the person who helps me the most as I continue on the path I'm currently on.

Sean didn't know what to say. He stood up and gave Kieran such a hug. When I think back, I don't actually think he bought him that pint, but he didn't need to.

Leadership Lesson – Ridiculing Others

Ensuring that leaders do not ridicule others as they climb the professional ladder is crucial for several reasons, both ethical and practical. Unfortunately, in this day and age, this still needs to be said.

Here are some of the key points why this matters:

- **Maintaining Respect and Dignity:**
  Leadership inherently involves guiding and influencing others. When leaders ridicule others, they compromise the fundamental respect and dignity that should be afforded to every individual. This behaviour can erode trust and morale within an organisation, making it difficult to foster a cooperative and positive work environment.

- **Building Positive Relationships:**
  Leaders who refrain from belittling others are more likely to build strong, positive relationships with their colleagues and subordinates. These relationships are essential for a collaborative and effective team. Positive relationships also facilitate open communication and feedback, which are crucial for organisational success.

- **Reputation and Legacy:**
  A leader's reputation is significantly influenced by how they treat others. Leaders who are known to ridicule their peers or subordinates

may gain a negative reputation, which can follow them throughout their careers, potentially limiting future opportunities. Moreover, a negative leadership style can become part of a leader's legacy, overshadowing other accomplishments.

- **Modelling Behaviour:**
  Leaders set the tone for organisational culture and norms. When a leader ridicules others, it may signal that such behaviour is acceptable, potentially leading to a toxic workplace environment where disrespect and humiliation are commonplace. Conversely, leaders who demonstrate respect and kindness encourage a culture of mutual respect and positivity.

- **Impact on Productivity and Creativity:**
  Teams led by supportive and respectful leaders are more likely to be productive and innovative. When team members fear ridicule, they may be less likely to take risks or propose new ideas, stifling creativity and progress within the organisation.

- **Legal and Ethical Consequences:**
  In some cases ridiculing others can lead to allegations of harassment or discrimination, which carry serious legal repercussions for both the individuals involved and the organisation. This can lead to costly legal battles, settlements, and damage to the organisation's public image.

Consequences of Ridiculing Others

The consequences of leaders who engage in ridiculing others can be far-reaching:

- **Loss of trust and respect:** This can lead to reduced loyalty and commitment from team members, which impacts team cohesion and effectiveness.

- **Increased turnover:** Employees are more likely to leave an organisation where they feel disrespected or undervalued, leading to higher turnover rates and associated costs for recruitment and training.
- **Poor morale:** Negative leadership behaviours contribute to a decline in morale, which can pervade the workplace and impact productivity and job satisfaction.
- **Damage to professional relationships:** Leaders who ridicule others may find their relationships with peers, subordinates, and even superiors strained, which can limit their effectiveness and advancement.

In conclusion, it is crucial for leaders to maintain a respectful demeanour towards others as they advance in their careers. The benefits of doing so are not only seen in the immediate health of the team but also in the long-term success and sustainability of the leader's career and the broader organisation.

The most important thing I've learnt over the years has been that nobody likes to sit in the company of someone who is either constantly negative or is always talking negatively about other people – I've done it, and after I learnt this lesson, I regained many friends and have never looked back.

Eleanor Roosevelt, wife of US President Franklin D Roosevelt once said, 'Great minds discuss ideas. Average minds discuss events. Small minds discuss people"'. As a leader, you need to have at least an average mind; call it a pre-requisite, if you will, however you should always strive to be great, and there's nothing to stop you from being so.

Seriously, other than personal feelings, if you have a problem with someone because of their behaviour in the workplace that does not involve the actual work, let it go the first time, speak to them directly and in private the second time, and if it is not well received or the bad behaviour continues, send it up the chain.

Otherwise, if you've nothing nice to say, believe me, none of us want to hear your voice. Do us all a favour, and keep it shut...you may end up doing yourself a favour in the long run. It's always better to have a voice that's unheard, than a voice that spews garbage.

Throughout the night as Sean recalled every second of his experience, and we dissected everything that did go wrong and the horrific possibilities of what may have happened, a strange feeling came across us. As all the other members of the club joined us and each one of them expressed their delight in the fact that Sean was still with us, we suddenly found ourselves right in the middle of the full group. Even though we'd been members of the club for nearly 2 years, that night I met other members for the very first time. We all found ourselves sharing Sean's experience and this was an experience that no skydiver ever wanted to go through; and this tale of survival brought us all together.

As a small group, my friends and I had kept ourselves apart, but this one experience tore all of that down, and for one night, we were all together as one big community. Except for one person who sat up at the bar on his own for most of the night. Sean spotted him and went to talk to him; the reason being that this was the person who packed the reserve parachute that was in Sean's rig. I can't remember his name, but in every club there is a person who is called a senior rigger; we'll call him Michael for this story, and his job was to pack the reserve parachutes. There are probably only 6 or 7 senior riggers in Ireland right now (back then probably fewer) and these people have done extensive training and completed certifications to perform this task as the impact of error is catastrophic. The reserve parachute is used as a last resort and is only used if the main parachute malfunctions.

Michael spent his evening sitting at the bar on his own and when Sean saw him, he thought he'd better go up and buy the man a drink. Now the funny thing is, it was Sean's reserve that didn't open, but Sean never even thought about that; he just saw Michael on his own, which was unusual because Michael was usually a very sociable character, and wanted to include him.

I didn't go with Sean but he told me this story afterwards. When Sean approached Michael and asked him if he would have a drink, Michael just looked at him and turned away. Sean asked him if he was ok, and his response was "You should be dead now. If you'd just done what you were told to do, you'd be dead now, and it would have been my fault. Just leave me alone".

And he was right. As mentioned previously, if Sean had followed the instructions exactly how they had been taught to us, he would have followed the 'Look-Locate-Peel-Punch-Pull', which means he would have **look**ed to **locate** the handles, **peel**ed away the release handle, **punch**ed it to release the main parachute (when they say punch, they mean punch away from your body...not punch yourself), and **pull**ed to open the reserve parachute. If Sean had done this, by the time he realised that the reserve had malfunctioned, the connections between the rig (harness) and the main parachute would have been severed, therefore when he opened the main parachute, and it would have just floated away into the air leaving him with nothing.

What Sean actually did was something that hadn't been taught to us because we were students. This is something that is taught as you progress further though your skydiving training, but certainly not at this stage, because it can confuse things. Also, it is extremely rare that a reserve parachute malfunctions.

Sean insisted that Michael have a drink with him and the two of them stayed at the bar together for a while. Michael was extremely upset with himself and was still in a bit of shock. Michael took his responsibility as the only senior rigger in the club very seriously and knew the consequences of any errors that he could possibly make. "You know, every time a main parachute malfunctions in this club", Michael told Sean, "I know that the person is cutting away confident in the knowledge that the reserve I packed will work and will save their life". He continued, "I sit here each weekend it happens, and I see the person who packed that malfunctioning parachute get the opportunity to apologise to the student, buy them a drink and promise that they'll do better next time. And every time I see that happen, I think, if the reserve parachute I pack malfunctions, I won't get that opportunity, and I've no idea how I would deal with that".

Sean tried to make light of this and tried to cheer Michael up by saying that everything worked out in the end, but Michael continued, "before we go on, let me buy you a drink. Your reserve malfunctioned up there today and you've survived to tell the tale, so the least I can do is buy you a drink. I have no idea why it malfunctioned, but I can promise you this, I will find out what I did wrong, and I will be better next time".

As they enjoyed a few drinks together, Michael told Sean about the checks and double checks that need to be done when packing a reserve, and that every reserve needs to be repacked every six months when it hasn't been deployed. The one in Sean's rig had just been packed a couple of weeks earlier which meant that it would have remained in that rig for another 5 months or so, and everyone who used that rig during that period of time would have had no idea that the reserve wouldn't work. The thoughts of anyone using that rig over the next few months and needing to use the reserve was terrifying.

Starting the following day, Michael started repacking ever reserve on the drop zone. He started with the student rigs and as the weeks went on, the progressed to the other rigs until he'd completed them all. He reinforced all the checks that were already in place and designed new checks, to second guess the checks and the double checks.

I bumped into him a few weeks after he had completed this massive task, and he said, "I still have no idea what happened with Sean's reserve, so all I can think of is that I must have missed something. The biggest challenge in skydiving has always been complacency, as the more and more you do something, the more confident you get and because we are all human we attempt to find ways to speed up the process. I don't think that's what happened. I don't think I took short cuts, but I don't know. The one thing I do know however is I will never get away with it like that again. So, I've repacked them all, I've implemented new checks to ensure I don't become overconfident and complacent, and I've learned a valuable lesson about myself. Sometimes we all need a kick in the arse to wake us up a little, and I got away with it by the skin on my teeth; your friend Sean gave me that kick and I made a promise to him a few weeks ago...and I won't let him down".

I thought to myself...perhaps this would be a good time to ask him whether he could smell the farts yet, but I decided that I'd prefer not to get a punch in the face in response! I did giggle a little about the thought though!

Still to this day, complacency is often cited as a significant issue in parachute clubs around the world. An issue they all have in common and an issue they continuously work to eradicate.

*"Complacency is a continuous struggle
that we all have to fight."*

– **Jack Nicklaus**

CHAPTER 14

THE REFLECTION

On reflection of everything that had happened during my skydiving journey, there were so many lessons that I had learnt. Perhaps I had not recognised them at the time, but I certainly do now. In the many years that have followed, it's been truly amazing how many times I've returned to this place and time in my life and looked at who I had been, and who I am now.

I would love to say that during my time as a leader of people over the past 25 years across numerous industries and sectors made me the leader I am today, but alas, that wouldn't be true.

The past 25 years in organisations has challenged the very core of my being; I have met some fantastic leaders, and some not so fantastic; and unfortunately, some absolutely horrendous leaders. The pressure to adapt to others' ways of thinking because of the need for a pay cheque can challenge even the best of us, however, being true to yourself is so important. And I know that's so easy to say; we all need that pay cheque.

Some of the lessons we are taught in leadership come from the most unusual places, and in a lot of cases, they do not come from boardrooms or the office floor or the people management courses we enrol on – they come from real life experiences.

As you read through the last few pages of this book, please think to yourself, how many of these skills were taught to you in a business setting?

I remember someone saying to me years ago, "It's not possible for a manager to manage teams across different industries and sectors; they need to understand everything about the service or product, or they won't earn the respect that's needed, and they need industry experience to learn that". I replied simply stating that a good leader leads the people, and whatever the industry or sector, people still have the same expectations and requirements from their leader – the setting is irrelevant. Remember: the greatest football managers are rarely the best footballers. It's how they inspire and motivate the team that matters. The knowledge and expertise in the product or service remains within the team, and they will always be the experts in this area; it's the leaders role to ensure that they know this and are appreciated for it.

Leadership Lesson – Take Time to Reflect

Taking the time to reflect on lessons learned from one's own life is profoundly important for leaders in several ways:

- **Self-awareness:**
  Reflection helps leaders understand their strengths and weaknesses, beliefs, and biases. This self-awareness is critical for effective leadership as it influences decision-making, and the way leaders interact with their team.

- **Empathy and Relatability:**
  When leaders are reflective they are more likely to empathise with their team members. This can enhance their ability to connect on a personal level making them more approachable and trustworthy.

- **Adaptability:**
  By reflecting on past experiences leaders can better adapt to new challenges. Understanding what worked or did not work in the past can guide their strategy and decision-making in future situations.

- **Role Modelling:**
  Leaders who demonstrate the importance of reflection are also teaching their team the value of learning from their own experiences. This can create a culture of continuous improvement and learning within the team.

- **Strategic Thinking:**
  Reflection allows leaders to step back from the day-to-day operations and think strategically. Understanding the broader impact of their actions and decisions can lead to more effective and thoughtful leadership.

- **Innovation and Problem Solving:**
  Leaders who reflect on their experiences are more likely to develop innovative solutions. By considering different perspectives and learning from past outcomes they can approach problems in new and effective ways.

Overall leaders who engage in personal reflection are likely to be more effective in guiding their teams, fostering a positive work environment, and achieving organisational goals. This practice not only benefits their personal growth but also significantly impacts their ability to lead others successfully.

But here are the problems:

- We don't take time in our lives to truly reflect on these events and the impact and relevance that they may have in other scenarios,
- We don't step back and take a high-level view of what just happened, what may have prevented it and how we can use these lessons in other situations,
- We react to the matter at hand, and then we forget about it, happy in the thoughts that, 'Gosh, we solved that one' or 'Wow, that was a close one', and we move onto the next crisis,
- And on, and on, and on.

And we're all the same. I have spent many years doing the very same as everyone else, and only when I took the time for myself to reflect on past experiences and measure the impacts and relevance that these experiences have taught me, and truly understood them, I was able to transition these lessons into other situations and adapt as necessary. In fact writing this book has been a huge journey on enlightenment for me. Never before in such detail have I truly listened to my own thoughts and 'rethought' them. I view this in myself as a process of change management, that change being the change in the person who I have become over the years.

You deserve it and owe it to yourself to reflect on the events and people in your life that have made a difference to you: the person you are now and the person you are becoming, and that includes the great influencers and the poor ones. Each had a lesson to teach.

As in leadership and business, people are in an ever-moving process of change management, and whilst we attempt to be so engrossed in adhering to the specific change management methodologies and principles in the projects we are involved in, we rarely use these principles when realising that we too are changing, and we are changing more rapidly than any project that I have ever been involved in.

Applying principles of change management to personal leadership development involves a systematic approach to identifying what needs to change, implementing those changes, and evaluating their effectiveness. Here's how you can use these principles to enhance your self-awareness and leadership effectiveness:

Awareness and Identification of Change Needs

- **Self-Assessment:** Regular self-assessment helps in identifying strengths and weaknesses. Tools such as 360-degree feedback, personality tests, or simply reflecting on past experiences can be invaluable.
- **Environmental Scanning:** Stay aware of the changing demands in your leadership role. This might include changes in team dynamics, organisational goals, or industry trends, which could necessitate changes in your leadership style.

Planning the Change

- **Set Clear Objectives:** Define what success looks like for the changes you want to make. This could involve improving certain skills, altering behaviours, or achieving specific leadership outcomes.
- **Develop an Action Plan:** This should outline the steps needed to achieve your objectives. Consider training, mentoring, and possibly reallocating your time to focus on areas of improvement.

Implementing the Change

- **Step-by-Step Approach:** Implement changes gradually and manageably. Breaking down changes into smaller, actionable steps can help make the process less overwhelming and more achievable.
- **Seek Support:** Engage mentors, coaches, or colleagues who can provide guidance and feedback as you implement changes. Their perspectives can help you adjust your approach as needed. Engage in opportunities for enlightenment outside the workplace, seeking resources such as seminars, classes, books, videos, and retreats.

Monitoring and Evaluating the Change

- **Feedback Loops:** Establish regular check-ins on your progress. This could be through formal reviews or informal feedback from peers and team members.
- **Reflective Practice:** Regular reflection on what's working and what isn't helps to refine your approach. Keeping a journal or diary can be a practical tool for this reflection as it allows you to not only observe your behaviour objectively but look back over time and see your progression.

Adjusting and Reinforcing the Change

- **Adaptation:** Be prepared to adapt your change strategies based on what you've learned from the feedback and your own reflections. Flexibility is crucial in responding to what is or isn't working.
- **Reinforcement:** Continuously reinforce the changes that have proven effective. This could involve further training, revisiting your successes in team meetings, or setting new goals that build on your improvements.

Practical Tips for Applying Change Management to Personal Leadership

- **Be Transparent:** Openly communicate about the changes you are trying to make with your team and yourself. This transparency not only sets an example but also opens up avenues for support and constructive feedback.
- **Maintain Consistency:** While flexibility is important, consistency in applying the changes you decide on is crucial for them to become habitual.

- **Use Technology and Resources:** Utilise available tools and resources, such as online courses, books, and workshops, to support your learning and change process.

By utilising these change management principles, you not only improve your own leadership skills but also set a positive example of adaptability and continuous improvement for you and your team. This approach not only leads to personal growth but also enhances the overall performance of you, your team and your organisation.

Yes, while it does seem a little unusual using such principles on yourself, it's entirely the same thing as bringing personal experiences into the realm of your professional life, except vice versa. As a leader it's so important to be authentic these days, and authenticity does not come from anywhere else than from within you and the lessons you have learnt in your personal life. And this authenticity was not learnt within a certain organisation or from a certain leader you admire (you can't allow them to take that from you), it comes from you, whether you know it or not.

The experiences that I have learnt whilst skydiving translate directly into my experiences in leadership, and over the years I have been in a very lucky position to be able to transition these learnings to help me grow and help others around me to do the same. And what helps more is that the others around me who I have imparted these learning to, realise that these are true authentic experiences, and after reflection have become true and relevant lessons for the world of leadership.

Authentic leadership is crucial because it builds trust, promotes transparency, and fosters a strong, positive organisational culture. However, leaders often struggle with authenticity due to several challenges:

- **Pressure to Conform:** Leaders may face pressure to conform to existing corporate cultures or leadership norms, which may not always align with their personal values or leadership style.
- **Fear of Vulnerability:** Being authentic means showing vulnerability at times, which many leaders fear could undermine their authority or lead to criticism.
- **Complex Stakeholder Expectations:** Leaders often have to balance conflicting expectations from various stakeholders, which can make it difficult to remain consistent and true to one's values.
- **Lack of Self-Awareness:** Some leaders may lack the self-awareness necessary to understand their values and how their actions align with these values. This can lead to behaviours that are perceived as inauthentic.
- **Changing Roles and Responsibilities:** As leaders rise through the ranks, their roles and responsibilities evolve, which can lead to challenges in maintaining their authentic self while adapting to new roles.

While authenticity is a powerful trait for leaders, maintaining it can be challenging due to external pressures, internal fears, and evolving responsibilities. Leaders can overcome these challenges by continually engaging in self-reflection, seeking feedback, and committing to personal and professional growth that aligns with their core values.

It's so important to recognise these challenges and ask yourself, is this who I really am? And how do I show my real self? Although your organisation has given you the position of authority, does that make you a leader?

Simon Sinek, author of *Find Your Why: A Practical Guide to Discovering Purpose for You and Your Team*, talks about the difference between leadership and authority and how having authority does not make you a leader. Simon says, 'Leadership has nothing to do with rank'.

The only thing that your organisation can provide you with is the authority. People will do as these leaders say because of the authority, 'but we would not choose to follow them. The rank itself is not what makes you a leader, it just gives you a leadership position'. (Sinek)

I have worked for many people who shouldn't be in the position of leader, but unfortunately have been provided with the authority – I would guess that most of us have. And it's a shame. And it's not always their fault.

Organisations might end up placing the wrong people in leadership positions due to a variety of reasons, often stemming from systemic issues, oversight, or a lack of proper assessment mechanisms. Here are some key factors:

- **Misalignment of Skills and Roles:** Sometimes individuals are promoted based on their performance in non-leadership roles without adequate assessment of their leadership skills. Success in one area does not necessarily translate to effectiveness in a leadership capacity.
- **Lack of Proper Assessment:** The selection process might not adequately measure key leadership competencies, such as emotional intelligence, decision-making capability, and ability to motivate and manage teams. Often a leader will be brought in from another company because of the growth that company experienced under that leader. However, the leader's methods, motives, and personality or leadership style may be unacceptable regardless of their ability to make money for the company.
- **Bias and Favouritism:** Decisions might be influenced by personal bias, favouritism or office politics, rather than based on objective criteria and performance metrics.
- **The Peter Principle:** This principle suggests that people in an organisation tend to be promoted based on their performance in their cur-

rent role, rather than on their abilities relevant to the intended role. They rise to their 'level of incompetence' and then no longer perform effectively. This can happen to you too, so be careful when accepting a role of leadership if you feel you are not ready. It's easy to accept a promotion, but then it's even easier to fall into the trap of others who have come (and gone) before you.

- **Short-Term Focus:** Organisations may prioritise immediate results over long-term potential, selecting leaders who can deliver quick wins instead of those who are better suited for long-term strategic planning and team development.
- **Lack of Development Opportunities:** Without sufficient training and development, individuals may not be prepared for leadership roles, even if they possess the potential to be effective leaders.
- **Cultural Misfits:** Sometimes, leaders are chosen without considering how well they fit with the company's culture, which can lead to poor team cohesion and organisational alignment.

Understanding these pitfalls can help organisations refine their selection and development processes for leaders, aiming to place the right people in the right roles for better overall outcomes.

And the trap that we sometimes fall into is to criticise these people rather than being true to ourselves and making the difference from where we stand. Another quote from Simon Sinek is, 'Be the leader you wish you had' – don't emulate a leader who you know if they are not up to your standard – don't criticise them... learn from them and their mistakes and be better. And if you have the strength, help them, but help them in a constructive manner. How do I do that? I hear you ask. It's different for everyone. Using your people management skills will help you with the individual person that you are dealing with. Remember, leadership does not just face downwards, it faces sideways and upwards too.

There are many ways to recognise a bad leader, and I'm sure most of you will have seen these in the people you've worked for. I hope too that some of you will recognise some of these traits in yourself and take the opportunity to reflect and make the relevant changes to improve yourself. There is always time, and at my age I find that I am constantly in a transition mode. I learn from so many different aspects of life, and I always ensure that I am open to change.

Identifying the characteristics of a bad leader can help organisations and individuals understand what to avoid in leadership roles. Here are some common traits associated with ineffective leadership:

- **Poor Communication Skills:** Ineffective leaders often struggle to communicate their vision, expectations, and feedback clearly and effectively. This can lead to misunderstandings, lack of direction, and demotivation among team members.
- **Lack of Vision:** A leader without a clear and compelling vision fails to inspire or guide their team towards strategic goals. This can result in stagnation and a lack of purpose within the team.
- **Inflexibility:** Bad leaders often resist change and new ideas, sticking rigidly to old ways even when they are no longer effective. This can stifle innovation and adaptation in a rapidly changing environment. It can also manifest as a form of bullying or intimidation.
- **Poor Decision-Making:** Consistently making poor decisions or avoiding decision-making altogether can undermine a leader's credibility and the trust of their team. It can also lead to missed opportunities and operational inefficiencies.

- **Micromanagement:** Leaders who micromanage demonstrate a lack of trust in their team's abilities. This can lead to decreased autonomy and motivation, stifling professional growth and innovation.

- **Lack of Empathy and Emotional Intelligence:** Ineffective leaders often fail to recognise or respond appropriately to the needs, feelings, and wellbeing of their employees in the name of the bottom line. This can result in low morale, high turnover rates, and a toxic workplace culture.

- **Failure to Develop Others:** A bad leader often overlooks the importance of developing their team, focusing instead on short-term goals or purely focussing on themselves. This neglect can lead to skill gaps in the team and hinder succession planning.

- **Ethical and Integrity Issues:** Leaders who lack integrity and do not adhere to ethical standards can compromise the entire organisation's reputation and morale. This includes engaging in dishonest behaviours, violating company policies, or treating people unfairly.

- **Self-Centeredness:** Leaders who are overly focused on their own achievements, recognition, and power often fail to support their teams effectively. They might prioritise their own interests over the well-being or success of their team. Remember, a great leader works for the team, and not the other way around.

- **Ignoring Feedback:** A leader who dismisses or ignores feedback can miss important opportunities for personal and organisational improvement, creating an environment where employees feel undervalued and unheard.

These characteristics can profoundly impact an organisation's culture, employee engagement, and overall effectiveness, making it crucial to identify and address poor leadership traits effectively.

And there's one that isn't mentioned above that I find close to my heart. When I initially thought about writing a leadership book I had an idea that I thought would clearly sum up all the lessons that a leader needed to have in their toolkit. I had planned that the book should be approximately 300 pages long, and each page of the book had only one line which said, 'Please refer to the front cover' – the book was going to be about a leader called Rick, and the title of the book on the front cover would be, 'Don't be a dick, Rick!'. I thought that would be a great start for some of the leaders we have out there, but my publishers thought I needed a slight bit more detail. I believe the lesson is still very valid, but I understood their point.

When I think about the many leaders I have worked for in the past, I have tried to emulate them, I have tried to present myself as they did, and I have copied the mistakes that they've made. I have also occasionally thought to myself, perhaps this leadership thing is just not for me because that's not the kind of person I want to become. But the one thing I forgot was about reflecting on me and who I am. I should have tried to emulate the best me, tried to present myself to others as me and learnt from my mistakes.

It's so important to run your own race and be yourself. When you get that first promotion into a leadership position, please trust that the reason you received that promotion was possibly not because of the experience you had at that time, but because of the person that they recognised in you – the person who would learn, the person who would be empathic and authentic, the person who would care about others ahead of themselves, the person who would represent the organisation in a professional and personable manner, the person who would trust others and be ethical and honest, and a person with a vision of not just the organisation of the future but a vision of themselves for the future.

The final reflection from my skydiving days takes me back to why I never really achieved the goals I had set for myself in the beginning, and the more I think about it, the more I place the reason for this on one thing: the incident Sean had.

That is not to say that I blame Sean in any way for my lack of success, but the impact his actions had on me were certainly a detrimental factor. As I listened to his story and I thought about all of the corners that he cut, the truths that he would not share with us and purposefully hid from us so that he didn't hinder his own progression, and the lack of self-awareness he had at that time and such poor decision-making which allowed him to do something so dangerous that it nearly cost him his life, I recognised myself in him, and I knew that it would have been so easy for me to have done the same. To be honest, I had never even thought about those corners and how they could have been cut, but if I had been in the position he had found himself, if I had been struggling to keep up and if I was making mistake after mistake, I recognised that my competitiveness would certainly have been a factor that could have guided me down the same road Sean had taken.

Every jump I did after Sean's incident caused more and more uncertainty in myself and my abilities. Every time I sat in the plane on my way up to altitude, I questioned everything about everything, but most importantly, I questioned myself about myself. Perhaps I was doing what Sean had done, perhaps I was hiding it from myself and others and perhaps I was so caught up in my progression and the goal I wished to achieve that I was unaware of it. I had already realised previously that my confidence and eagerness to succeed had been clouding my judgment when it came to recognising the severity of the activity I was doing, and potentially this was a part of me that would cause me to do something stupid. And in this line of sport or activity, doing something stupid will not usually provide you with an option to apologise and try again. Sean was lucky and got that opportunity – his apology was to himself, and he never tried again.

Leadership Lesson – Remember the impact of your actions on others

In leadership, you always will have the opportunity to apologise and try again. I sometimes wish that Sean had apologised to me for his actions because they had a subconscious impact on me, and it's only whilst writing this book that I realise this. If his behaviour had not resulted in such an almost catastrophic event, I may have probably kept going in my skydiving journey and possibly would have achieved my goal. But the blame sits firmly with me. I allowed the impact of Sean's decisions to affect my future and that's the one thing I regret the most.

Sometimes we come across people who are in leadership positions, and we ask ourselves, how on earth did that happen? And sometimes the actions of these people cause discontent within a team, which they may not be aware of but you can see, and sometimes the actions of these people cause discontent within the leadership team, which you can also see, and you think to yourself, 'Now, why would I want to be in that position?', and it deters you from achieving your goal.

As with Sean, I believe that he just wasn't ready and only did this because the rest of us were doing so. I believe that he hid his failings because he didn't want to get caught out. I believe he was being dishonest with himself, didn't ask for help and unfortunately in the world of skydiving, that can have serious consequences.

It's the same with many leaders; they see this promotion as a step up the ladder; they know they're not ready, but they're afraid that if they don't take the promotion, they'll be passed over; they hide their failings because they don't want to get caught out; they don't ask for help because they think this makes them look weak; but what they don't realise is that these behaviours have an impact on those around them. I cannot count the amount of times I've heard, 'No thank you, I just don't need that pressure in my life'; and it's usually said by the very people who would be excellent at leadership, who have already brought the core fundamentals of leadership to the table from their external experiences, and it's the behaviours of the people within the organisations who have muted their desire to achieve what they were perhaps built to do; every time I see this, I think, 'Wow, such a shame'.

Please, please, please...if you're not ready to be a leader, be honest with yourself and allow the opportunity to pass you by this time. There is no 'fake it until you make it' in leadership, because people are just not that stupid, and they'll see right through you. Give someone else the opportunity to shine while you get yourself ready, and once you're ready...go for it. You may not believe it, but if you're honest with your leadership team, they'll respect you more. And if you don't think so based on the experiences in your organisation...you're working for a leadership team who doesn't care about your future and growth. Run for the hills, my friend!

However, after all that has been said, perhaps Sean's experience probably saved me from having an even more catastrophic one of my own, and perhaps that is why I am here writing this book. We can never look into the future, and we can never second guess what happened in the past; however, we can learn from it and use that learning to become better people and better leaders.

Look after each other out there and thank you so much for reading this book. I hope that you can learn from the experiences that I have had and the lessons that I have learnt.

In the end, remember this: Don't be a dick, Rick.

ACKNOWLEDGEMENTS

First and foremost, I would like to acknowledge and sincerely thank all my friends who have contributed their stories and experiences to this book. Please note that the names mentioned in the stories have been anonymised to respect the privacy of those involved.

A special acknowledgment goes to the remarkable community at the Irish Parachute Club. Although the events described in this book occurred many years ago and might lead readers to think otherwise, I want to emphasise that safety was and always has been the top priority at the club. The environment back then might have seemed challenging, but nothing could be further from the truth in terms of the club's commitment to safety. Today, the Irish Parachute Club continues to uphold the highest standards, creating a safe, welcoming, and supportive environment for everyone who walks through its doors. It's still great craic too.

To all the instructors, staff, and fellow skydivers, your dedication and passion for this exhilarating sport have been inspirational, and I am grateful to have been a part of such a fantastic community. Your stories and the lessons learned from our shared experiences have been integral to the fabric of this book.

Lastly, thank you to the readers who embark on this journey with me. May the stories within these pages inspire, entertain, and remind you that with the right team, there is no limit to how high we can soar.

Printed in Great Britain
by Amazon

7d64f912-c8c1-45f6-85c0-3e1340bb9039R01